Designing Student Leadership Programs:

Transforming the Leadership Potential of Youth

Mariam G. MacGregor

3rd Edition
2005

Publisher: Youthleadership.com
Designing Student Leadership Programs: Transforming the Leadership Potential of Youth
Copyright © 2000 by Mariam MacGregor, Denver, CO
3rd Edition, 2005
Updated 2007

ISBN-10   0-9677981-6-7
ISBN-13   978-0-9677981-6-5

All rights reserved. No part of this book may be reproduced in any form or by any means, or stored in a database or retrieval system, without prior written permission of the publisher, except in case of brief quotations embodied in critical articles or reviews.

Youthleadership.com
5593 Golf Course Drive
Morrison, CO 80465
Ph: 303-358-1563
Fx: 303-393-9066

email: support@youthleadership.com
website: http://www.youthleadership.com

Table of Contents

Using this Book	5
Brief Overview of Leadership & Leadership Education	6
What is a Youth Leader	9
Trends in Youth Leadership	11
What's Missing for Youth Leaders	14
Youth Theories vs. Adult Theories	16
Defining Leadership	18
Adolescent Leadership Issues:	
Middle School (Early Adolescence)	21
High School (Later Adolescence/Young Adult)	24
Assessing Program Objectives & Potential for Success	29
Building a Foundation for Youth Leadership	32
Youth Participation in Your Current Program	36
Evaluating Your Current Program (Discussion Sheet)	39
Inventory of Adult Attitudes & Behavior (Lofquist & Miller)	41
Creating Nurturing Environments for Leadership Development	47
Designing an Integrated Leadership Education Program	51
Components of Successful Programs	52
Core Facets of Youth Leadership Development	54
Selecting/Developing Leadership Curriculum	56
Social Change Model of Leadership Development	58
The Leadership Challenge Model of Leadership Development	62
Self Evaluation for Youth Leaders	64
The Reflection Model	68
Debriefing and Reflection for Leadership Activities	70
Leadership Development as an Intervention Tool	73
Building Youth Leadership Self Confidence	76
Leadership Studies Content Standards	82
Leadership Across the Curriculum	85
Youth Leadership in the Community	92
Leadership in the "Real World"	97
Determining Reasonable Outcomes	99
Methods for Assessing Youth Leadership Learning Outcomes	102
Activities that Promote Leadership Development	107
Developing Your Skill as a Leadership Educator	109
What Adult Mentors Can Do	111
Inspiring Youth Leaders	113
Leadership Program Action Plan	114
Bibliography & Resources	117
Leadership Library	118
Organizations/Websites	125
Youth Leadership Conferences & Programs	136
Professional Development Opportunities	143
Movies to Use for Leadership Discussions	147
Leadership Action Plan (for teens)	148
Sample Leadership Project Evaluation (Self and Group)	149
About the Author	150

Designing Student Leadership Programs
Copyright © 2000 Mariam MacGregor
3rd Edition, 2005

Using This Guidebook

Designing Student Leadership Programs is the result of workshops I conducted for a number of years to prepare adults working with youth leaders. It is set up as a "guidebook" to be used within staffs or as part of discussions as your program or school evaluates or establishes your youth leadership program. This guidebook is based on my belief that youth deserve as much attention, preparation, celebration, and the resources to become leaders, as are dedicated to preparing business, political, and community leaders.

As a guidebook, there are pages that consist of lists of ideas and/or statements that have been gathered and tested in various youth leadership programs. There also are pages that consist of provocative questions to consider when establishing a program or evaluating your existing efforts. Obviously, the most effective way to use this book is with a group of people (adults and youth) rather than having only one person design your program.

Throughout the book are "Notes" pages to use for jotting down ideas and issues to consider. I strongly encourage using this book as you would a notebook...writing on the pages and keeping track of ideas. Often when undertaking a project -- and establishing a strong youth leadership program is a project -- we write our thoughts down or talk about them with others, but neglect to take action because the ideas somehow get lost. Using this book to gather all of the issues into one place can assist with streamlining your efforts.

Midway into the book, you will find brief outlines of two leadership models to use with youth. To fully understand their usefulness with your program, I encourage you to read the supporting materials for both (*The Social Change Model of Leadership* and *The Leadership Challenge*). These models were selected because, from my experience working with teens, they seem to connect easily with both these approaches. Youth leadership behaviors tend to be community- oriented, often emphasizing fairness, justice, and the common good. Youth leaders also can be very supportive of others on their "team" and work hard to include many people in accomplishing a goal. Each of these models captures these concepts within their framework. The details for supporting information for these models can be found in the bibliography section.

There is ample commentary that could accompany each page and activity in the book. I haven't included it so you can use the information as it relates to your specific efforts. Some pages may be interpreted slightly different in a school-based setting versus a community-based setting. Ultimately, the book is designed to prompt and challenge you to evaluate all aspects of preparing the youth with whom you work, as well as provide you with ample resources and ideas for successful implementation. Good luck with your efforts!

A Brief Overview of Leadership & Leadership Education

For years, Leadership often has been considered a product and necessity of business or management training. Much of the existing research and longitudinal studies, as well as anecdotal observations apply to the business world or other corporate environment. Max DePree, John Gardner, Stephen Covey, Margaret Wheatley, Barry Posner, Jim Kouzes, John Maxwell ...these are all recognized names in the field of business/management based leadership. Many of their theories easily can apply to community-based and educational leadership. These theories also provide a starting point for developing comprehensive and effective youth leadership programs. *Youth leadership* is one of the fastest growing interest areas in the field of leadership development, with programs being developed in schools and communities world-wide.

For years, expectations of young leaders often have been higher than the training provided for them to succeed in their leadership roles. Student leaders, particularly at the middle and high school levels are put into positions of leadership through popular vote, teacher/staff selection, or parental urging. Frequently, students in leadership roles have little in-depth understanding of the significance of their role or the personal development that come with the experience. Many of my interviews with youth leaders indicate that experiences would be much more meaningful if someone had taken the time to explore what being a leader meant to them and how to get the most from a particular leadership position. In addition, teen leaders frequently express that not everyone is interested in being in student council, yet often, those students are the only ones given opportunities to take leadership classes or participate in leadership workshops or trainings.

Secondary educators, youth group leaders, community youth development programs and other youth leadership avenues at times lack consistent and deliberate connection between the youth leadership experience in their program and the application of these skills to the real world. Because of this, some youth leadership experiences remain stagnant or superficial in truly promoting youth empowerment and leadership ability. Many teens also begin to perceive their leadership experiences -- athletics, student government, youth group, clubs, school participation, class involvement, or volunteering -- as "fun and games" without connecting them meaningfully to daily life. In cases where leadership is part of a "turn around" program (diversions, intervention, etc.), youth may even participate because they feel they *have* to, rather than participating to enhance personal development.

At the college level, the sophistication and integration of leadership development has increased tremendously over the past fifteen years. The advent of these programs increases the expectation that college-bound students be sufficiently prepared to take on the responsibilities of involvement in college leadership opportunities.

For secondary students who do not attend college, the increased quality of college leadership efforts reinforces the need for sufficient preparation at the middle and high school level. As students enter adulthood, they will find themselves working with an increasingly diverse and complex workforce. When competing with college educated peers who have been exposed to multiple leadership development options, the difference for professional success will be evident in how capable each person is at being a leader within their own field and with colleagues.

Surprisingly, comprehensive leadership education for adolescents is not something that is built into most curricula. And although many activities of adolescence contribute to positive leadership development, these activities frequently take place without concentrating efforts on discussion, debriefing, application, and mastery. For example, a student who is elected to lead their student council may recognize the power of their new position without recognizing how capable or prepared s/he is to carry out that position. Unfortunately, many advisors may not have time to conduct appropriate leadership training in order for youth to be prepared as a leader, yet we expect that youth leader to demonstrate consistent and balanced leadership abilities!

Recognizing that youth need assistance in identifying, developing and fine-tuning leadership skills is our first step. Recognizing that youth leadership is different than adult theories of development is also an important step [See Josephine A. van Linden & Carl I. Fertman's book *Youth Leadership* for research support]. The challenge becomes how to dedicate time and energy to developing leadership skills and sensitivities in youth. Rather than viewing leadership as qualities that one "either has or doesn't" and treating adolescents as such, it is increasingly important to recognize that every teen has the potential to be a leader. It is equally important to recognize what our roles and our abilities are in helping every teen develop their leadership abilities to this potential.

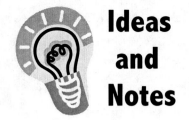

Ideas and Notes

What is a Youth Leader?
(Brain storm with your group)

_____
_____
_____
_____
_____
_____
_____
_____
_____

Here are some responses from youth leaders with whom I've worked:

- Believes in themselves
- Stands up for what they believe
- Learns how to communicate
- Appropriately confronts others when needed
- Demonstrates acceptable behavior both with peers and adults
- Listens to others
- Possesses qualities of responsibility, trustworthiness, dependability, ethical decision making skills, ability to compromise, tolerance and sensitivity to people different than themselves, among other things
- Recognizes their ability to positively contribute to their community
- Works with peers and adults to find solutions for problems
- Does not use violence to solve problems
- Makes mistakes and learns from them
- Tries to learn from each activity, whether successful or not
- Values the opinions of others
- Does no harm
- Just and fair with others
- Does not know it all and is willing to learn
- Takes on responsibility and follows-through

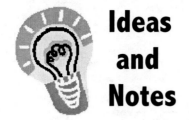
Ideas and Notes

Concepts of Youth Leadership

Trend	Outcome
Philosophical Approaches rather than Specific Theories	Youth develop individual and personal beliefs about leaders and leadership instead of attempting to fit into leadership categories
Organized Leadership Development Efforts	Youth have similar experiences as their peers and can apply these experiences to their daily life. School and community programs are closely linked
Fundamental Qualities of Leaders	Youth become capable of recognizing their own strengths and challenge areas as leaders. Youth also become more savvy in identifying acceptable and appropriate standards for socially recognized leaders
Selection Criteria	Youth are expecting more from peers who are elected or selected into leadership roles. In situations where this criterion is loose or compromising it results in poor youth leaders and peer/adult dissatisfaction.
Youth Participation	Youth have opportunities to take on increasingly responsible leadership roles in school or the community. Youth are increasingly sought out for their opinions by community agencies and political figures (Mayors, Senators, & City Councils) when decisions will directly affect youth "quality of life"
Diversity and Sensitivity to Differences	Youth are taught to celebrate social values of diversity and tolerance and to recognize their responsibility to these issues when serving as leaders. The natural ability to lead also is considered by some researchers as an indicator of giftedness in Latino and African-American boys. Modern leadership

	styles, in education, community, and business, are more representative of "feminine" developmental models. Asian cultures tend to identify and nurture leadership abilities from very young ages
Generation Gap	Youth experiences are increasingly recognized and valued for their complexity and difference from previous generations
Peer Mediation and Intervention Programs	Youth are given identified and peer-respected leadership roles to assist peers in developing personal power and control in daily conflicts
Mentoring Programs	Youth are increasingly encouraged to seek out (or are set up with) mentors within their school or community. More adults are taking on mentorship responsibilities to contribute positively to the adolescent experience
At-Riskness	All youth are recognized to possess some "at-riskness" and programs are developed to address these issues without treating them as "abnormalities" or unable to be overcome. Integrated and across the board leadership development contributes to empowering at-risk youth rather than further segregating teens into cliques. Youth identified with factors of being "at-risk" are the highest growing population of youth yet is often overlooked for in-depth leadership development.

Notes and Ideas

What's Missing for Youth Leaders?

- Youth leaders are given few opportunities to "make mistakes" without having it held against them

- Appropriate contemporary social role-models

- A sense of being valued for their present experiences rather than wanting them to "grow up"

- Consistent leadership standards from parents, teachers, and other close adults

- Leadership development efforts that reflect how leadership skills apply in daily life and for the future

- Sensitivity to the power of pre-adolescence and adolescence experiences

- At-risk youth often are overlooked for school-related leadership roles. In turn, negative social experiences take precedence (e.g. gangs, negative peer-pressure, adult acquaintances, drug culture, etc.)

- Sensitivity to diversity and cultural differences as youth leaders

- Adult mentors comfortable with empowering youth and allowing youth to take on significant responsibilities and leadership roles

- At times, the inability to envision the difference and power of one person or a small collective of individuals

- Consistent, frequent opportunities to take on leadership roles within the communities or organizations most influential to youth (e.g. schools, youth groups, community centers, etc.)

- Flexibility to learn from spontaneous classroom or group discussions - many efforts are "over-programmed" and "climate-controlled"

Notes and Ideas

Youth Leadership Theories and How They Differ from Adults!

(Collected from individual interviews and based on held beliefs before a person participates in a leadership education/development program)

Youth	Adults
Caring for others is an important demonstration of your leadership abilities.	Stoicism and perseverance is often rewarded.
Standing up for what you believe in, whether expressed appropriately or not.	There is a time and place for everything.
Leaders are good looking and popular! Only good kids are good leaders.	Leaders are good looking and popular! Good business people are good leaders.
Leaders are born, if you are going to be a leader you must have something special about you.	Leaders can be made. Hard work and having others follow you can help you become a leader.
Others respect you for the risks you take, whether appropriate or not.	Risk taking is necessary for all leaders...but there are limits and appropriate types of risk.
Confronting authority and changing the "system" is important.	Understanding the role of authority and ways to negotiate "the system" is important.
Adults do not value the opinions and perspectives of youth as they relate to leadership roles and decisions in society.	Adults do not value the opinions and perspectives of youth as they relate to leadership roles in society.

Designing Student Leadership Programs
Copyright © 2000 Mariam MacGregor
3rd Edition, 2005

Notes and Ideas

Defining Leadership

There is no better place to start than with establishing an agreed upon definition of leaders and leadership!

(Instructions: In small groups, brainstorm the following, writing the terms/phrases on newsprint. Hang the newsprint up and have each group share/comment on their words. Debrief/discuss as appropriate)

When you hear the word "Leader" or "Leadership" what words come to mind? In addition, what do you hope people are thinking when they refer to you as a leader?

Defining Leadership (Continued)

Reflecting on your words above and those shared by the group, write below your personal "working" definition of leadership.

_____
_____
_____
_____
_____
_____
_____
_____

How do you communicate or model this definition to the youth with whom you work? Be specific.

_____   _____
_____   _____
_____   _____
_____   _____
_____   _____

Write (3) significant leadership experiences you shared with a teen (where you acknowledged how the youth's behavior related to leadership). Be specific.

1) _____
_____
_____

2) _____
_____
_____

3) _____
_____
_____

Notes and Ideas

Adolescent Leadership Issues

Middle School Leadership

The following leadership efforts should be progressive - that is, each new grade in school should build upon the previous years. What is learned, practiced, and applied in meaningful ways in sixth grade relates to seventh grade, and likewise, to eighth grade. These skills also prepare young leaders for high school/later adolescent leadership roles and activities.

6th Grade
(11 - 12 years old)

The significant "leadership-related" issues facing Sixth Graders include: social well-being, fitting in, adjusting to middle school, making new friends, peer pressure, finding identity, determining personal values, and learning the value of education. They are still concrete thinkers and see things as "right or wrong". They are still willing to play!

Leadership development should focus upon:

Developing Identity - Values - Self Esteem/Self Worth
Developing Confidence - Communicating with Others
Boundaries & Rules/Standards
Team Building - Value of Education - Social Issues
"Becoming a Leader" - Refusal Skills
Standing Up for Your Beliefs - Diversity/Differences

7th Grade
(12 - 13 years old)

The significant "leadership-related" issues are similar to sixth grade and also include: "middle kids" of middle school, finding identity, testing limits, trying new things, boy/girl relationships, changing roles of friends, sex, drugs, social pressure, friends versus family (autonomy), diversity issues. These students need to know how to get help for personal issues or to deal with different situations.

Leadership development should focus upon:

Developing Identity - Values - Self Esteem/Self Worth
Communicating with Others - Self-Confidence
("I'm Okay, You're Okay")
Team Building - Social Issues - Setting Boundaries/
Understanding Limits — Dealing with Bullies
Value of Education - Refusal Skills
"What Kind of Leader Am I?"
Standing Up for Your Beliefs - Diversity/Differences
Getting Along with Others - Dealing with Cliques/Fitting In

8th Grade
(13 - 14 years old)

The significant "leadership-related" issues include: trying to be "cool", popularity, acting out or being overly shy (extremes in behavior), proving yourself, taking unnecessary risks, negative peer pressure (drugs, alcohol, sex, etc.), transition into high school, self-esteem, working with others, confusion, emotional troubles (depression, loss, suicide)/self worth, diversity, the value of education, and developing independent study habits. Eighth graders can be excellent role models for younger kids. They can also lose interest in school if they fear the transition to high school. A struggle also starts between being a "little teenager" to being like the "big teenagers." Leadership and social issues can be presented with increasing abstractness.

Leadership development should focus upon:

Communication Skills - Team Building - Self Esteem
Decision Making - Refusal Skills – Dealing with Bullies
Rivalry versus Diversity - Transition to High School
Taking Life & Choices Seriously - Boundaries
Appropriate Risk Taking - Role Modeling
Self Expression/Independence - Managing Emotions
Growing Up - Power/Authority/Influence

Other Leadership Issues for Middle School:
- Finding role models/mentors
- Shifting relationships with teachers or other significant adults
- Clear distinctions between male and female developmental issues
- Accessing assistance or help for personal issues
- For eighth graders, being "top dogs" in the school
- Peer Pressure!
- Understanding how one "fits" into society
- Wanting to be older than one's age

High School Leadership

High school leadership roles and responsibilities are quite different than middle school. Often, middle school experiences do not adequately prepare high school students for the true potential of the leadership experiences they can have as they get older. Just like middle school, high school leadership development is progressive, that is, what is learned at each stage is built upon for the following stages.

9th Grade
(14 - 15 years old)

The significant "leadership-related" issues facing Ninth Graders include: establishing identity and autonomy, conflict resolution, communicating with others, responsibility, locus of control (consequences), diversity, high school "hierarchy", planning for the future, developing confidence, leading an organization/club, changing leadership roles (sports, music, arts, academics, etc.), shifting roles with friends, conflict of friends and family, peer pressure, managing stress, maintaining interests, and the value of education.

Leadership development should focus upon:

Developing Identity - Values - Self Esteem/Self Worth
Developing Confidence - Communicating Skills - Credibility
Team Building - Value of Education - Social Issues
"Becoming a Leader" - Working with Others
Standing Up for Your Beliefs - Delegating to Others
Running Meetings - Diversity/Differences - Creative Thinking
Taking Responsibility - Handling Stress - Goal Setting

10th Grade
(15 - 16 years old)

The significant "leadership-related" issues facing Tenth Graders are similar to 9th grade, although becoming a bit more complex, including: conflict resolution, communicating with others, responsibility, locus of control (consequences), diversity, high school "hierarchy", planning for the future, developing confidence, leading an organization/club, changing leadership roles (sports, music, arts, academics, etc.), leading friends (as members of organizations or teams), peer pressure, managing stress, maintaining & balancing interests, and the value of education.

Leadership development should focus upon:

Developing Identity - Values - Being a Role Model
Developing Confidence - Communicating Skills - Credibility
Team Building - Value of Education - Social Issues
"Becoming a Leader" - Working with Others
Standing Up for Your Beliefs - Delegating to Others
Running Meetings - Diversity/Differences - Creative Thinking
Taking Responsibility - Handling Stress - Goal Setting

11th Grade
(16 - 17 years old)

The significant "leadership-related" issues facing Eleventh Graders include: taking on leadership roles with organizations; balancing friends, family, work, and school; speaking out; involving others; value of education; post-graduation planning; relationships; balancing enjoyment with responsibility; community involvement; respecting the choices of others; motivation; conflict resolution; making effective decisions; delegating to others (maintaining balance); entering "young adult" status; dealing with stereotypes; setting and communicating goals; dealing with consequences (at higher level), reflecting and maintaining respect; increasing autonomy with family; balancing budgets; and following through on commitments.

Leadership development should focus upon:

Establishing Identity - Prioritizing - Getting/Giving Respect
Developing Confidence - Communication Skills - Credibility
Team Building - Value of Education - Social Issues
Follow-through and Responsibility - Working with Others
Standing Up for Your Beliefs - Delegating to Others
Running Meetings - Diversity/Differences - Creative Thinking
Staying Motivated - Handling Stress - Time Management
Public Speaking Skills - Goal Setting/Creating Vision
Planning for after High School - Getting & Keeping a Job
School to Career Relationships - Problem Solving
Making Ethical Decisions - Applying Life Skills

12th Grade
(17 - 19 years old)

The significant "leadership-related" issues facing Twelfth Graders include: balancing responsibilities with school, work, family, and friends; taking on significant leadership roles with various organizations; planning for after high school; academic pressures; setting goals; changing status of relationships; standing up for beliefs with increasing depth; legal voting process and participation; "young adult" status; increasing autonomy and independence from family and community; membership and participation within community; making long-term choices; balancing monetary commitments; modeling the way for others; leaving home or living on own; motivation; and managing stress.

Leadership development should focus upon:

Demonstrating Identity - Setting Priorities
Developing Confidence - Communication Skills - Credibility
Value of Education - Social Issues - Community Leadership
Working with Others - Budgeting - Conflict Resolution and Appropriate Confrontation Skills - Staying Motivated
Standing Up for Your Beliefs - Delegating to Others
Diversity/Differences - Creative Thinking - Balancing Choices
Taking Responsibility - Handling Stress - Voting Information and Being an Informed Citizen - Relationships
Post Graduation Planning - Goal Setting/Creating Vision
School to Career Connections-
Study Skills & Time Management

Notes and Ideas

Assessing Program Objectives & Potential for Success

Allow each individual the time necessary to complete this "survey" prior to discussing as a group. It is often useful to pass it out prior to the session to allow thoughtful consideration by each participant.

- What are the values of your organization related to developing youth leaders?

- Does your organization see an ongoing need for youth leadership development?

- In what ways does youth leadership development enhance the goals of your organization?

- What youth leadership development efforts currently exist in your school/ organization?*(If None, see Section A Below)*

- Who began these efforts? Is that person still with your organization?

- Is leadership development tied directly to the person who started (or who is responsible for) the leadership efforts or are they integrated through out your program, regardless of the person currently responsible for them? *(If Yes, see Section B Below)*

- How do youth and staff respond to these efforts...that is, are they supported, participated in, valued, etc.?

- Who are the allies/supporters to these efforts? Are these allies in decision making positions?

- What are the politics around these efforts? That is, what are your motivations for offering youth leadership development opportunities?

- How are these efforts funded? Are these funding sources long-term?

Section A
No Leadership Education Efforts Currently Exist:

- Would the youth you serve say the same thing?
- How are you defining leadership?
- What is the underlying mission of your organization? Is there a "missing link" between what your organization stands for and what your organization is really doing?!
- Is funding or staffing limited, or preventing your organization from promoting "proactive" programming?

Section B
Leadership Development is tied directly to the person who started (or is responsible for) leadership efforts:

- What are the values of your organization? Is youth leadership development one of them? How are these communicated to all staff members?
- How are staffing responsibilities assigned?
- Is there territorialism overshadowing the overall needs of youth who access your organization's services?
- Are you understaffed or inefficient in connecting/linking subject matter or youth development efforts? (The reality is that leadership development can be linked to EVERYTHING!)
- If the person left, *and your organization values youth leadership development,* what is your plan for sustaining your leadership efforts?
- What steps can be undertaken to prevent the loss of your current leadership programs? *(That is, how can you begin to integrate youth leadership development throughout your program efforts?)*

Notes and Ideas

Building a Foundation for Youth Leadership in Your Program

Leadership development efforts for youth should not be approached haphazardly. Instructors or facilitators of youth leadership programs should identify the following significant factors in evaluating and contributing to the success of designing meaningful youth leadership programs and experiences:

What theory (ies) of leadership do you embrace?

- Philosophical
- Structural
- Positional
- Situational
- Cultural
- Traditional
- Eclectic

How does this theory fit with your youth population? Have you considered:

- Culture
- Race
- Socio-Economic Status
- Gender
- Identity
- Social
- Values/Beliefs
- Age

What social issues currently and significantly impact your youth population (what is their reality)?

How do youth currently demonstrate/exhibit leadership abilities in your program/school?

How are they recognized (or chastised) for exhibiting these skills? (Be honest)

What outcomes do you desire for your youth population?

Are these outcomes the same ones youth associated with your program expect or hope for?

What steps need to take place to achieve that outcome? Are they reasonable and attainable?

How informed are you to contribute to that outcome?

How are you motivated to contribute to that outcome?

How empowered are the youth (both within your organization as well as in the neighborhood in which they live or other influential "communities")?

What is *your* (personal) relationship with your youth population?

Write below, in a few sentences, what you would like the **Mission Statement** or **Vision** of your organization's youth leadership development program to be:

_____
_____
_____
_____
_____
_____
_____

How will you know if this Mission or Vision has been accomplished?

What measurements will be used to determine the success of your youth leadership program?

How will these measurements be communicated, promoted, and advocated throughout your organization and/or the community?

When you present this outline to youth in your organization, what will they say?

When you present this outline to adults in your organization, what will they say?

Notes and Ideas

Youth Participation - Evaluating Your Current Program

To make this activity most effective, you should have youth and adults complete it in separate groups; then bring groups together to discuss and apply.

1   2   3   4   5   6   7   8   9   10

On the line above, with (10) being "Always" and (1) being "Never" (or (10) being "Many" to (1) being "Zero"), do the following:

- ☐ Draw a SQUARE around the number which represents how youth are involved in the development of your school's or organization's policies (specifically, policies which directly effect youth)

- ○ Draw a CIRCLE around the number which represents how many youth live in your surrounding community

- ◆ Draw a DIAMOND around the number which represents how youth are involved in the development of leadership efforts which directly impact them

- ✓ Put a CHECK on the number which represents how youth are involved in staff or teacher selection for your school/organization

- ✗ Put an X on the number which represents how youth are valued in Your State

In the space below, list any organizations or groups which you believe have found ways to involve young people in the planning, operation, and evaluation of their programs: _____
_____
_____
_____
_____

What is it about that organization that makes you believe they actively involve youth? (What have you heard, what does the organization promote, what have you experienced, etc.?) _____
_____
_____
_____
_____

How do you think your school, organization, or program compares?

       Worse   The Same   Better   Exceptional

List some reasons why...Be specific: _____
_____
_____
_____
_____

How can you use this activity to positively change or enhance youth participation in your organization? _____
_____
_____
_____
_____

Notes and Ideas

Evaluating Your Current Program

Discussion Group

(In small groups, discuss and take notes. Share with larger group and debrief/ discuss further as appropriate. If possible, have groups with a mix of youth and adults)

A. Barriers to Youth Participation:

B. Benefits of Youth Participation:

C. Dangers of Not Involving Your Youth:

D. Action Steps (Make them Specific and Attainable)

This activity adapted from The Technology of Prevention Workbook

 **Notes and Ideas**

Inventory of Adult Attitudes & Behavior: An Instrument for Examining the Nature of Adult/Youth Relationships

William A. Lofquist & Martin G. Miller, Ph.D.

This inventory is designed to give adults who work with young people an opportunity to consider their approach to their work. It is based upon an assumption that attitudes are closely related to behavior and that by examining attitudes it is possible to make sound decisions about how one can best shape an organization's approach to relating to young people.

The statements below explore various aspects of the processes of planning, operation and evaluation the work of youth focused organizations. To what extent are young people involved in these processes, and how do the attitudes and behaviors of adults within the organization affect the relationships of young people with the organization and with regard to accomplishing the processes. Young people can participate in using the Inventory by indicating how well the statements describe the approach they see adults in the organization taking. This youth perspective can be quite valuable.

The Inventory includes 24 statements. The respondent is to select the number from the opinion scale and place it in the space provided to the left of the statement. The use of numbers from the lower end of the scale indicates that the statement is UNLIKE the way the respondent approaches things. The use of numbers from the upper end of the scale indicates the respondent uses an approach SIMILAR to the statement.

OPINION SCALE

1   2   3   4   5   6   7   8   9

Never my Approach	Seldom my Approach	Sometimes my Approach	Often my Approach	Always my Approach

STATEMENTS

_____ 1. As an adult leader, I engage young people in program decisions when I think this engagement will be a growth experience for them.

_____ 2. It is most appropriate that adults determine what the programs for young people will be.

_____ 3. Young people have a vantage point that is valuable for evaluating the successes and failures of specific programs.

OPINION SCALE

1	2	3	4	5	6	7	8	9
Never my Approach		Seldom my Approach		Sometimes my Approach		Often my Approach		Always my Approach

_____ 4. Training programs designed to improve organizational effectiveness should teach adults how to encourage young people to accept the organization's expectations, processes and programs as adults have designed them.

_____ 5. Adults can share carefully selected management roles with those youths who are ready to learn, under close adult supervision, from the experience.

_____ 6. Young people are encouraged to assume leadership responsibility within a youth/adult partnership in carrying out youth programs.

_____ 7. In our organization decision making, adults should make the decisions.

_____ 8. I believe that allowing young people to participate in organizational roles can open valuable learning opportunities for them.

_____ 9. As an adult leader, I engage young people in making program decisions at the earliest point.

_____ 10. Asking young people to review adult-determined program plans will communicate to the young people that the adults respect them.

_____ 11. Adults are in the best position to evaluate the successes and failures of a specific program.

_____ 12. Training programs designed to improve organizational effectiveness should teach adults how to engage young people's participation in those organizational decision processes that will help the young people learn to make more responsible decisions in real-life situations.

_____ 13. Youth participation can enhance and enrich the various management roles within our organization.

_____ 14. Fewer mistakes are made in carrying out a program for young people if adults perform the leadership roles themselves.

_____ 15. Adults should allow young people to participate in making decisions that will provide learning experiences for them.

OPINION SCALE

1　2　3　4　5　6　7　8　9

| Never my Approach | Seldom my Approach | Sometimes my Approach | Often my Approach | Always my Approach |

_____ 16. I believe that experiences of young people give them a valuable perspective that can become useful in efforts to plan, operate, and evaluate the way the organization functions.

_____ 17. As an adult leader, I seldom ask for the opinions of the youth participants when I make program decisions.

_____ 18. If young people are active participants in the planning process of an organization, they can help make the program more relevant to their needs and desires.

_____ 19. Asking the opinions of young people as part of program evaluation will help them sharpen their thinking and observational skills.

_____ 20. Training program designed to improve organizational effectiveness should teach adults how to foster young people's participation in decision processes to bring the perspective of young people to bear on improving the organization.

_____ 21. Management roles within our organization, by their very nature, are adult roles.

_____ 22. Allowing young people to assume some leadership roles can help them develop skills for the future.

_____ 23. In our organizational decision making, adults and young people together should make the decisions.

_____ 24. I believe that allowing young people to participate in organizational decision making would mislead them into thinking they can influence matters beyond their control.

Now that you have completed the Inventory, the results can be tabulated by using the form on the next page.

This inventory and the following interpretive pages are printed with permission of Development Publications, Tucson, AZ.

Inventory of Adult Attitudes & Behaviors Scoring Instructions

Transfer the numbers given to each statement in the Inventory to the appropriate box. Total the numbers at the bottom in each column to determine your ranking for each style.

Statement	STYLE #1	STYLE #2	STYLE #3
1		____	
2	____		
3			____
4	____		
5		____	
6			____
7	____		
8		____	
9			____
10		____	
11	____		
12		____	
13			____
14	____		
15		____	
16			____
17	____		
18			____
19		____	
20			____
21	____		
22		____	
23			____
24	____		
TOTAL POINTS:	_____	_____	_____
RANK:	_____	_____	_____

What the Styles Mean

Style #1
Youth Viewed as Objects

The basis of this attitude is that adults "know what's best" for youth. Or adults may decide they have the right to determine the circumstances under which youth or youth groups may exist. Youth who are viewed and treated as objects usually know it. This style expects young people to conform to the program and the adults involved have no intention of allowing true youth involvement and participation in designing or executing programs.

Style #2
Youth Viewed as Recipients

Here the adults still believe they know what is best for youth, but they "give" youth the opportunity to participate in decision making because it will be "good" for the youth. Thus, youth are supposed to receive the benefits of what adults give to them. The adults in this case are still in control and although this style does allow increased effectiveness of the programs, youth are still aware that their opinions and contributions have certain "boundaries" on how they are used.

Style #3
Youth Viewed as Resources

Here there is an attitude of respect by the adults toward the youth, and vice versa. This attitude and the behaviors which follow it can be closely associated with two matters of great concern in youth: self-esteem and productive contributions to the community. Creating a culture in which youth are viewed as resources is a worthy goal, resulting in increased organizational or programmatic effectiveness and personal growth of both youth and adults involved.

Notes and Ideas

Creating A Nurturing Leadership Development Environment

Nurturing	**Controlling**
Youth feel free to share their opinions and ideas on leadership	Youth are hesitant to share their opinions and protect themselves from criticism
All ideas are okay and encouraged	Adult mentor guides topics and controls outcomes
Personal leadership growth is more important than "performance"	Leadership "performance" is more important than personal leadership growth & learning
All leadership subjects/issues are open for discussion and brainstorming	Adult mentor controls and leads discussions or brainstorming
Individual youth differences welcomed	Youth are expected to and accepted conform to strongest person's ideas (or to the ideas of adult mentor)
Each youth is responsible for own actions	Youth are shamed or put down for actions
The group values and develops skills for respectful feedback and appropriate consequences for actions	Control and perfectionism takes precedence and feedback becomes criticism
Few "shoulds"	A lot of "shoulds"
Clear and flexible rules or boundaries on discussing and learning about leadership	Unclear, inconsistent, & rigid rules or expectations about what leadership is
Atmosphere is relaxed and cooperative	Atmosphere is tense and competitive
Learning about leadership is fun and enjoyable	Learning about leadership is stressful and burdensome

Creating A Nurturing Leadership Development Environment

Nurturing	**Controlling**
Youth are capable of facing and working through stress as leaders	Youth avoid stress or become overwhelmed when taking on leadership roles
Youth have energy and excitement about being leaders	Youth are exhausted and over-programmed as leaders
Leadership opportunities and experiences are spread around to many youth with diverse perspectives and skills	The same youth are relied upon over and over, with very few chances for other youth to take on leadership roles or demonstrate their skills
Youth leaders feel valued and important	Youth leaders feel hurt, disappointed, and unimportant
Personal growth is celebrated, even if mistakes are made along the way	Personal growth is discouraged and taking appropriate risk is avoided so that no mistakes will be made
Youth have high self-worth	Youth have low self-worth
Youth and adult mentors create a positive and productive coalition	Hierarchy exists between youth and adult mentors
Leadership is a shared journey between youth and adult mentors	Leadership is a road which is directed by adults and paved by youth
Adult mentors advocate for youth and the possibilities of their leadership accomplishments	Adult mentors downplay the possibilities for youth leadership successes

Notes and Ideas

Designing an Integrated Leadership Education Program

Integrated Leadership Education

Integrated Leadership Education implies that youth leadership experiences are connected to nearly everything they do. By incorporating leadership concepts across academic curriculum, in service projects, through daily discussion, within school-to-career initiatives and in community activities, youth are exposed to the wide-range of positive possibilities related to being a leader (or taking on leadership roles). Ultimately, approaching leadership education as an *integration of experiences* contributes to developing "citizen leaders" of all youth -- individuals who conduct themselves as leaders, whether or not others are around.

Components of Successful Programs

- Involving Youth!

- Making the Leadership Experiences Meaningful and Valuable to All Parties (avoiding having youth undertake projects "just for the experience" of it)

- Setting the "bar" high. Refraining from underestimating what youth leaders can do and how resilient youth can be

- Being clear about your standards and asking youth about theirs!

- Identifying *your program* parameters and sticking to them. Do not try to develop the leadership skills of every adolescent with whom you come in contact!

- Flexibility & timeliness of experiences and leadership development efforts

- Clearly identifying goals for the leadership efforts

- Sensitivity to diversity. Consistently incorporating and addressing culture, class, gender, and other diversity issues which directly affect youth

- Organizational support to conduct leadership development for all youth in your programs

Notes and Ideas

Integrated Leadership Education
Core Facets of Youth Leadership Development

Leadership Knowledge
(The Concept or Philosophy of Leadership)

What do youth KNOW about leadership?

What can they LEARN about Leadership?

What characteristics are important for Leaders?

Leadership Skills & Sensitivities
(The Ability to Lead)

What strengths and abilities do youth possess?

What skills can they learn? How can they learn them?

What sensitivities can they learn? How can they learn them?

Specific for your program:
What do you <u>want</u> them to learn?

Leadership Competence
(The Application & Practice of Leadership or Leading)

What experiences exist for youth to apply their
leadership knowledge, skills and sensitivities?

How can these experiences be sustained and enhanced?

What opportunities exist to continue to build on knowledge & skills?

Notes and Ideas

Integrated Leadership Education

Selecting/Creating Meaningful Leadership Curriculum

Suggestions for each area (of "core facets"):

I. Basic Leadership Knowledge

> Defining Leadership
> Identifying Characteristics of Leaders
> Identifying Individuals with Leadership Capacity
> Identifying Personal Skills (Talent Inventory)
> Determining a Philosophy of Leadership

II. Leadership Skills & Sensitivities

> Working with Others (Team Building; Group Dynamics)
> Resolving Conflict/Conflict Resolution
> Appropriate Confrontation
> Communication
> Understanding Power, Influence, Authority
> Tolerance & Diversity
> Decision Making (Ethical; Situational; Group; Individual)
> Building Consensus
> Delegation Skills
> Appropriate Risk Taking (Leadership-based)
> Ability to Think Creatively

III. Building Competence

> Putting Words into Action
> Leadership Projects
> Experiential opportunities
> Reflection & Feedback
> Abstract/Global Application

Notes and Ideas

Integrated Leadership Education
Social Change Model of Leadership Development

This model incorporates several key assumptions:

- "Leadership" is concerned with effecting change on behalf of others & society

- Leadership is **collaborative**

- Leadership is a **process** rather than a position

- Leadership should be **value-based**

- **All students** (not just those who hold formal leadership positions) are potential leaders

- **Service** is a powerful vehicle for developing students' leadership skills
  ("Service" describes activities that serve the common good)

(page 10, A Social Change Model of Leadership Development: A Guidebook, Version III)

Leadership development can be examined from three different perspectives or levels:

The Individual

○

The Group

○

The Community/Society

Integrated Leadership Education

The Social Change Model of Leadership identifies Seven Core Values as the elements of the model:

- **Collaboration**
- **Consciousness of Self**
- **Commitment**
- **Congruence**
- **Common Purpose**
- **Controversy with Civility**
- **Citizenship**

The "hub" of the model (around which the model was developed):

Change

Organized within the three levels of the model:

Individual Values
Consciousness of Self
Congruence
Commitment

Group Values
Collaboration
Common Purpose
Controversy with Civility

Community/Societal Values
Citizenship
Change

Integrated Leadership Education

Social Change Model Definitions of Core Terms

Consciousness of Self: Being aware of the beliefs, values, attitudes, and emotions that motivate one to take action.

Congruence: Thinking, feeling, and behaving with consistency, genuineness, authenticity, and honesty toward others. Congruent individuals are those whose actions are consistent with their most deeply-held beliefs.

Commitment: The energy that motivates an individual to serve and that drives the collective effort (team). Commitment implies passion, intensity, and duration. Knowledge of self is fundamental to commitment so that the commitment is not misdirected!

Collaboration: To work with others in a common effort. It capitalizes on the multiple talents and perspectives of each group member and on the power of that diversity to generate creative solutions and actions. Collaboration empowers each individual best when there is a clear-cut "division of labor"

Common Purpose: To work with shared aims and values. Recognizing the common purpose and mission of the group helps to generate the high level of trust that any successful collaboration requires.

Controversy with Civility: This recognizes two basic realities of any creative group effort -- that differences in viewpoint are inevitable, and that such differences must be aired openly but with civility. Civility implies respect for others, a willingness to hear each other's views, and the exercise of restraint in criticizing the views and actions of others.

Citizenship: Where the individual and the collaborative group become responsibly connected to the community and society through the leadership development activity. To be a good citizen is to work for positive change on behalf of others and the community.

Change: The ultimate goal of the creative process of leadership -- to make a better world and a better society for self and others.

Summarized from A Social Change Model of Leadership Development: A Guidebook. *Higher Education Research Institute, University of California, Los Angeles.* Available from the National Clearinghouse for Leadership Programs (https://nclp.umd.edu/publications/index.asp)

Notes and Ideas

Integrated Leadership Education

The Leadership Challenge Model of Leadership Development

Challenging the Process
- Search for Opportunities
- Experiment and Take Risks

Inspiring a Shared Vision
- Envision a Future
- Enlist Others

Enabling Others to Act
- Foster Collaboration (working together)
- Strengthen Others

Modeling the Way
- Set an Example
- Plan Small Wins

Encouraging the Heart
- Recognize Individual Contributions
- Celebrate Accomplishments

From *"The Leadership Challenge: How to Get Extraordinary Things Done in Organizations"* by James Kouzes and Barry Posner (Jossey Bass)

Notes and Ideas

Integrated Leadership Education
Self-Evaluation for Youth Leaders
(Another Useful Way to Guide Your Program)

Think about your relationships with others, your skills in helping and leading others (as individuals and in groups), and what you bring to being a leader. Then:

- *Read through the list of characteristics/activities and decide which ones you are doing the right amount of, which ones you should do more of, and which ones you should do less of. Make a check for each item in the appropriate place.*
- *Some goals that are not listed may be more important to you than those listed. Write those goals on the blank lines; and*
- *Go back over the whole list and circle the numbers of the three or four activities which they want to improve most through your leadership participation, activities, and experiences.*

Communication Skills:	Need to Do Less	OK	Need to Do More
1. Talking in the group	_____	_____	_____
2. Being brief and concise	_____	_____	_____
3. Being forceful	_____	_____	_____
4. Drawing others out	_____	_____	_____
5. Listening Actively	_____	_____	_____
6. Thinking before I talk	_____	_____	_____
7. Keeping my remarks on the topic	_____	_____	_____
8. _____	_____	_____	_____

Observation Skills:	Need to Do Less	OK	Need to Do More
9. Noting tension in the group	_____	_____	_____
10. Noting who talks to whom	_____	_____	_____
11. Noting interest level of the group	_____	_____	_____
12. Sensing feelings of individuals	_____	_____	_____
13. Noting who is being "left out"	_____	_____	_____
14. Noting reaction to my comments	_____	_____	_____
15. Noting when the group avoids the topic	_____	_____	_____
16. _____	_____	_____	_____

Problem-Solving Skills:

	Need to Do Less	OK	Need to Do More
17. Stating problems or goals	_____	_____	_____
18. Asking for ideas, opinions	_____	_____	_____
19. Giving ideas	_____	_____	_____
20. Evaluating ideas critically	_____	_____	_____
21. Summarizing the discussion	_____	_____	_____
22. Clarifying issues	_____	_____	_____
23. _____	_____	_____	_____

Morale-Building Skills:

	Need to Do Less	OK	Need to Do More
24. Showing interest	_____	_____	_____
25. Working to keep people from being ignored	_____	_____	_____
26. Helping people reach agreement	_____	_____	_____
27. Reducing tension	_____	_____	_____
28. Supporting the rights of individuals in the face of group pressure	_____	_____	_____
29. Giving praise or appreciation	_____	_____	_____
30. _____	_____	_____	_____

Expressing Emotions:

	Need to Do Less	OK	Need to Do More
31. Telling others what I feel	_____	_____	_____
32. Hiding my emotions	_____	_____	_____
33. Disagreeing openly	_____	_____	_____
34. Expressing warm feelings	_____	_____	_____
35. Expressing gratitude	_____	_____	_____
36. Being sarcastic	_____	_____	_____
37. _____	_____	_____	_____

Facing & Accepting Emotional Situations:

	Need to Do Less	OK	Need to Do More
38. Facing conflict & anger	_____	_____	_____
39. Facing closeness & affection	_____	_____	_____
40. Handling silence	_____	_____	_____
41. Facing disappointment	_____	_____	_____
42. Dealing with tension	_____	_____	_____
43. _____	_____	_____	_____

Social Relationships:

	Need to Do Less	OK	Need to Do More

44. Competing to outdo others
45. Acting dominant/better than others
46. Trusting others
47. Being helpful
48. Being protective
49. Calling attention to myself
50. Standing up for myself
51. _____

General:

	Need to Do Less	OK	Need to Do More

52. Understanding why I do what I do (insight)
53. Encouraging comments on my own behavior (asking for feedback)
54. Accepting help willingly
55. Making up my mind firmly
56. Criticizing myself
57. Waiting patiently
58. Balancing many things to do and knowing when I am over my head.
59. _____
60. _____

 **Notes and Ideas**

Integrated Leadership Education
The Reflection Model

The scheme below represents the process of moving from initial experience to reflecting upon the experience and applying it to one's greater sphere of influence. Begin the circle at "Experience", which represents the initial moment, activity, discussion, etc. that one goes through which challenges or causes wonder regarding previously held beliefs. Move through the circle going clockwise through disequilibrium and so on. This model can be applied on a small level (i.e. in activity debriefings) as well as on a large level (i.e. addressing issues with great societal consequence).

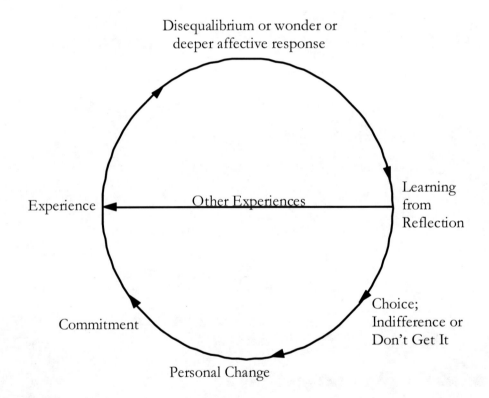

Used with Permission from Santa Clara University – Center for Student Leadership

 **Notes and Ideas**

Integrated Leadership Education
Debriefing and Reflection for Leadership Activities

Important first steps:

- Create a safe/comfortable environment (set up "ground rules" if appropriate)
- Respect everyone's chance to share or be quiet
- Know your role as a leader (or facilitator of the discussion/reflection)
- "Attend" to others - in other words, pay attention to body language, group dynamics, and direction the group is going (or trying to take the discussion)
- Actively listen
- Ask open-ended questions
- Don't just talk to fill space...use silence for reflection time and thoughtfulness
- Include all in the discussion, prevent "talkers" from dominating

Sample Questions (Depending upon the topic or issues):

- How did you feel about this experience?
- What were the reasons behind it?
- What did you get out of this experience?
- What did you learn from this activity?
- What problems did we run into while trying to solve the problem?
- How did we get this goal accomplished?
- What did it take to get everyone to work toward the same outcome?
- What did you like about this activity? What did you dislike?
- What kind of example is this activity...that is, how can you apply it outside of this experience?
- What skills did you have to apply?
- What skills did you build?
- How does this activity/experience relate to real life?
- How does this activity/experience relate to leadership?
- Where do we go from here?
- Who/what stood out for you in the experience? Why?
- What expectations did you have about the experience/activity? Was it what you expected or not? How or in what ways?

- What advice would you give to people going through the same experience?
- Would you have done anything differently? If so, what?
- What did you learn about yourself through this activity?
- What did you learn about your group through this activity?

Ideas for Including All Group Members:

- Ask each participant to share one thing they learned, or respond to a specific question you ask of the group.
- Probe into each question further depending upon what responses are given.
- If the activity/experience addresses a specific topic or issue, ask questions or encourage discussions which go deeper into that issue.
- Encourage the group to build upon the answers of others (if appropriate).
- Always provide a "transition" from the activity to the way it applies in a greater sense to the lives or perspectives of the participants (both as individuals and as a group).
- Provide opportunities for participants to present their own reflection/debriefing questions or comments.
- Encourage youth to lead discussions and to contribute to ways to connect the experience to their activities in and out of the organization

Notes and Ideas

Sustaining Skills
Leadership Development as an Intervention Tool (Incorporating it on a daily basis)

Consider why leadership education/development can be a daily activity in most programs:

- Leadership behaviors are action oriented
- Leadership behaviors are present tense ("here & now") and to help youth prepare for their future
- Leadership behaviors are personal and individualistic
- Leadership behaviors become reinforced when youth work with others
- Leadership behaviors promote locus of control skills
- Leadership behaviors promote self-esteem and confidence
- Leadership behaviors combine thought, action, feelings, and physiological responses
- Leadership recognizes that there are various definitions of leadership yet common terms which apply to leaders and leadership
- Leadership skills can be taught, practiced, and improved upon
- People who desire to be leaders may have to make changes in their behaviors to become a leader

How can you incorporate leadership development into existing programs and within daily meeting times:

- Use leadership "language" with your students (the language of taking control and believing that you are valuable and important to others)
- Use leadership development activities as sessions for groups. Use debriefing and reflection which relates the experience to the issues of the group as well as to what they can do in their daily life
- Dedicate every other group session to "developing leadership"
- Depending upon the subject matter of individual sessions, begin to incorporate leadership skills development as part of your counseling "action plans " (or homework)
- Develop a leadership library from which youth can check out books or videos

- Show movies with leadership themes to your groups, discuss, and apply to the issues at hand
- Offer an organized, on-going leadership development class. Have this class offer consistent experiences for every student who completes it...as time goes on, the culture of your program will begin to reflect the ideals you develop in the class, regardless of when the student participated in the class!
- Within diversity sensitivity programs, communicate the importance for leaders to recognize and value diversity. Create activities which assist in developing these skills and sensitivities
- Acknowledge and recognize students who make good leadership decisions, both in their mental health, peer activities, and other involvements
- Create or enhance Peer Mediation Training and Follow-up
- Create youth review boards or "decision" committees to help with organizational decisions - Meet regularly!
- Develop a schedule for youth to bring in topics for leadership discussion from current events

Building Allies Across the Curriculum

- Leadership Education efforts add depth to the perception of affective development and activities
- Leadership classes can be co-taught with a counselor/social worker and curricular instructor
- Invite teachers/administrators to observe your students in action
- Promote the accomplishments of student leaders
- If you offer a leadership class or group (which focuses on developing leadership skills), rotate it in the academic schedule. Give teachers ample warning when students will be missing their classes for a leadership activity or conference
- Invite teachers to be co-sponsors and/or to accompany students who attend leadership conferences and workshops
- Relate leadership development efforts to the Counseling Content Standards or to Leadership Education Content Standards
- Have peer mediators or other "counseling-based" student leaders present at a faculty meeting or "School Improvement" meeting
- Encourage teachers/administrators to talk with students who have taken on leadership roles at school, especially with those students who have had a hard road getting there!

 **Notes and Ideas**

Sustaining Skills
Building Youth Leadership Self-Confidence

How you want youth leaders to feel   *What you can do to develop this*

SECURITY: a feeling of confidence. The person feels comfortable and safe and knows that he/she can count on you.

1. Build a trusting relationship
2. Be clear about your expectations & rules; make sure you are consistent
3. Create a positive & accepting environment

SELFHOOD: a feeling of self-knowledge. The person has accurate and realistic self-descriptions regarding their strengths, physical characteristics, and roles with others.

1. Give them chances to figure out accurate self-descriptions
2. Give them chances to discover their personal power
3. Build awareness of unique qualities
4. Help them identify & appropriately express emotions & attitudes

AFFILIATION: feeling like one belongs, is accepted, and can relate to others. A person achieves this feeling when they have relationships where the other person is important to them.

1. Make them feel supported & accepted when they are with you
2. Give them chances to discover the interests, strengths, and backgrounds of others
3. Increase their awareness in how to build friendships
4. Encourage peer approval & support

MISSION: feeling that one has influence & responsibility over situations in their life. Able to set direction for him/herself by setting realistic & achievable goals. Has a sense of purpose; gains self-motivation.

1. Help them improve their abilities to make decisions, explore alternatives & identify consequences
2. Help them "chart" leadership (past, present, future) & behavioral achievements
3. Help them learn steps to successful goal-setting

COMPETENCE: feeling successful in things which are personally important or valuable. Being aware of strengths & able to accept weaknesses.

1. Give them chances for success & ways to show their strengths
2. Teach them ways to check on their own progress
3. Give them feedback to help them improve where necessary and how to learn from mistakes
4. Teach & model "self-praise" for accomplishments

Integrated Leadership Education
Security

Indicators of Low Security

- Shows signs of stress or anxiety
- Uncomfortable with new experiences
- Has difficulty handling change or spontaneity
- Unsure of other's expectations
- Distrusts others
- Doesn't know who can be counted on or how to find out

Steps to Achieving Security

- Build a trusting relationship
- Set limits and rules that are consistently enforced
- Create a positive and caring learning environment

Activities and Strategies to Build Security:

Trust activities
- **Sharing activities**
- **Delegate responsibilities to youth**
- **Diversity Awareness activities**
- **Team building activities**
- **Ropes Course**
- **Balancing Your Lifestyle (Wellness Awareness) activities**
- **Identifying needs activities**
- **Appropriate Risk taking activities**

Integrated Leadership Education
Selfhood

Indicators of Low Selfhood

- Uncomfortable with their physical appearance
- Has difficulty accepting praise
- Conforms, follows, or imitates others
- Poor self-knowledge (identity)
- Feels inadequate
- Feels powerless in many situations

Steps to Achieving Selfhood:

- Give them chances to figure out accurate self-descriptions &
- ways to tap into sources of influence on self
- Build an awareness of unique qualities & abilities
- Help them identify & appropriately express emotions and
- attitudes.

Activities and Strategies to Build Selfhood:

- **Ice Breakers**
- **Setting Group Norms & Expectations**
- **Understanding Power activities**
- **Diversity Awareness activities**
- **Group Dynamics activities**
- **Ropes Courses**
- **Talent Inventory activities**
- **Self Identity activities**
- **Working with others; Committee membership**

Integrated Leadership Education
Affiliation

Indicators of Low Affiliation

- Relies on adults for companionship
- Withdraws, rejects, or isolates self
- Connects with objects or animals more than people
- Has difficulty starting and keeping friendships
- Doesn't understand the concept of friendship or hasn't experienced
- it for an extended time

Steps to Achieving Affiliation:

- Make them feel supported & accepted when they are with you
- Give them chances to discover the interests, strengths, and
- backgrounds of others
- Encourage peer approval & support

Activities and Strategies to Build Affiliation:

- **Team building activities**
- **Group dynamics activities**
- **Communication Skills development**
- **Making Decisions**
- **Talent Inventory activities**
- **Understanding Values activities**
- **Ropes Courses**
- **Strengths "Bombardment" activities**
- **Diversity Awareness activities**

Integrated Leadership Education
Mission

Indicators of Low Mission

- Cannot see alternatives or solutions
- Indecisive, feels powerless
- Overdependence on others for directions, structure, and encouragement
- Unmotivated, little initiative (ability to start things on own)
- Poor task completion
- Has a hard time evaluating their performance
- Poor goal-setting capabilities

Steps to Achieving Mission:

- Help them improve their abilities to make decisions, explore
- alternatives & identify consequences
- Help them "chart" present & past leadership & behavior
- performances and expectations
- Help them learn steps to successful goal setting

Activities and Strategies to Build Mission:

- **Decision making activities**
- **Ethics and Values activities**
- **Motivation activities**
- **Problem Solving skills development**
- **Conflict Resolution and Confrontation activities**
- **Project design activities**
- **Autonomy development activities**
- **Ropes Courses**
- **Power Issues activities**

Integrated Leadership Education
Competence

Indicators of Low Competence

- Can't or won't speak up on their ideas or opinions
- Fear of failure or mistakes
- Poor loser; can't accept weaknesses
- Gives up easily... "I can't" attitude
- Puts down their achievements
- Behavior "flares up" when they feel incompetent
- Has difficulty identifying strengths

Steps to Achieving Competence:

- Give them chances for success & ways to show their strengths by setting high standards and achievable expectations
- Teach them ways to check on their own progress
- Give them feedback to help them improve where necessary and how to learn from mistakes
- Teach and model "self-praise" for accomplishments

Activities and Strategies to Build Competence:

Problem Solving skills development
- **Strength "Bombardment"**
- **Talent Inventory**
- **Confronting perfectionism activities**
- **Presentation planning and skills development**
- **Committee membership and involvement**
- **Ropes Courses**
- **Motivation activities**
- **Communication skills activities**

Leadership Studies

Indicators of Performance

Sample Content Standards	1	2	3	4	5	6
1.1 Establish working definition of leadership	Establishes Common terms	Recognizes Good & Bad Qualities	Understands History of Leadership			
1.2. Identifies & Develops common leader characteristics	Identifies Well-Known Leaders	Recognizes Characteristics in Action	Identifies peers with leadership potential			
1.3 Identifies self-possessed qualities of leadership	Identifies strengths related to common terms	Analyzes how skills change when in leadership roles	Compares personal qualities with those of other leaders	Explains what terms apply to self and how to enhance abilities		
1.4 Recognizes role and expectations of leaders in society	Explains role of leaders in society	Identifies and evaluates historical leadership figures	Evaluates contemporary leadership figures and role in current events			
2.1 Identifies concepts linked to Leadership and Leaders	Defines Concepts of Power	Compares, Contrasts & Apply concepts of Authority & Influence	Identifies appropriate role-models	Demonstrates respect and integrity		
3.1 Capable of working cooperatively with others	Differentiates between Group & Team	Identifies characteristics of functioning teams	Creates & Recognizes Team Building Activities	Practices leading and participating in team	Sets Goals as Team	
3.2 Learns skills for communicating & listening	Defines characteristics of "communication"	Differentiates between hearing & listening	Defines "feedback" and constructive input	Demonstrates effective communication skills	Demonstrates active listening skills	Demonstrates and receives feedback
3.3 Recognizes relationship of followers in leadership	Identifies followership	Differentiates between followership & peer pressure	Understands group dynamics & hierarchy			
4.1 Learns to recognize & appreciate diversity	Defines Diversity & Tolerance	Identifies characteristics of Prejudice	Describes positive qualities of people different than self	Recognizes stereotypes and generalizations	Productively discusses controversial topics with peers	Constructs strategies for overcoming biases & prejudice

Mariam G. MacGregor, 2005

4.2 Understands role of leaders in diverse society	Identify diversity of well-known leaders	Identify own contribution to a diverse society	Communicate value of diversity	Evaluates own effect, as a leader, on others	
5.1 Able to show decision making skills and aspects of making sound decisions	Recognizes impact of decisions on others	Defines & Understands Ethics	Applies Ethical Decision making skills to all decisions	Recognizes impact of decisions & consequences	Explains how decision affects self & others
5.2 Knows and is able to accept responsibility	Describes responsibility & follow-through	Evaluates how respons. as a leader is sim/diff. to indiv. responsibility	Follows through on commitments		
5.3 Able to productively resolve conflicts and confront others	Demonstrates communication skills	Understands difference between consensus & majority rules	Productively discusses conflicts with others involved	Recognizes personal role in conflicts and takes responsibility for this role	Recognizes that conflict is good and can help group improve
6.1 Understands motivation, goal setting, and vision	Explains what motivates self	Understands various motivational theories	Capable of motivating others through various appropriate means	Develops plan for future of self and organization	Defines Vision and recognizes role of a leader in demonstrating vision to others
6.2 Understands role-modeling and mentoring	Able to stand up for beliefs	Differentiates between group think & moral independence	Recognizes impact of behaviors & decisions on others	Actions are consistent with standards of leadership & leading others	Understands and confronts unreasonable expectations of peers

Mariam G. MacGregor, 2005

Notes and Ideas

Integrated Leadership Education/Sustaining Skills
Leadership Across the Curriculum

Opportunities exist in every academic area to investigate, educate, and explore the topic of leadership. The following categories are brief examples of how leadership can appropriately and profoundly be incorporated into curricula without compromising the integrity of curricular standards.

Social Studies

Content Standards (Generalizations - Varies by District/State):

Chronology of people and events in history (U.S. & World)
Societal changes based on diverse cultures
Economics
Use and loss of political power through history
Origins/Development of philosophical & religious ideas
Democratic principals in U.S.
Use of and understanding maps, globes, other technologies
Definition and determination of regions
Ecosystems and environmental issues
Relationships between natural systems & human systems
Civics & society

Leadership Opportunities Within Social Studies:

- Concepts and discussions of diversity, tolerance, prejudice & social norms
- Ethical Decision Making
- The Philosophy of Leadership
- U.S. and World Leaders - Style, Impact on Society, Global Leadership
- Leadership Decisions and Environmental Policy
- Leadership and Spirituality
- Concepts, discussions, and projects related to social change and justice
- Service Learning Activities, Reflection, and Sustainability
- Autocratic, Democratic, Abdicratic Leadership & Societies
- Student tutors

Other: _____

Science

Content Standards (Generalizations - Varies by District/State):

Design and perform scientific investigations
Characteristics and interactions of living things
Change in organisms over time
Cycle of matter and movement/transformation of energy
Interactions of matter within a system
Historical development of scientific thought
Integration of sciences for key concepts, processes, procedures
Structure of solar system, universe and space exploration
Composition of earth, its history and processes that shape it

Leadership Opportunities Within Science:

- Application of ethics and ethical decision making
- Skills of investigation and abstract conclusions
- Concepts of diversity, extinction, and handling change
- Team building and collaborative skill building (lab partners; group work)
- Debate and public speaking skills (discussion of controversies in sciences)
- Investigating relationship and impact of cause and effect (responsibility and consequences)
- Leaders in science throughout history
- Contributions of scientific investigation in sociological reference (impact on greater society)
- International competition for space exploration "leadership" (or superiority); tracing exploration through time
- Dilemma and discussion on creationism versus evolution
- Debate over environmental conservation versus modern development (using Thoreau's Walden) and the role of leaders throughout history on this topic
- Peer tutors

Other: _____
_____
_____

English

Content Standards (Generalizations - Varies by District/State):

Writing process: grammar, mechanics, spelling, meaningful text
Comprehension skills of various materials (texts, techniques, structures, etc.)
Uses reading and writing to enhance thinking and understanding (with critical response skills)
Ability to research using various methods including analyzing own skills as reader and writer
Writing process to create meaningful text
Cultural attributes, contributions, and diversity
Understanding literary genres
Listening processes to receive, construct, and express ideas
Applying speaking process to construct/express ideas

Leadership Opportunities Within English:

- Leaders in Literature
- Study of heroes/heroines (fiction & non-fiction)
- Interpretation of well-known speeches by leaders
- Public speaking/communication development
- Oral debates
- Written reflection and research
- Autobiographical and Biographical readings, research, and investigation
- Conflict of fiction versus non-fiction in representing contributions of literary leaders
- Socratic seminar approach to English topics
- Communication skills and value of presenting information (strength of skills increasing how information is received by others)
- Utilizing/analyzing "Letters to the Editor" as expressions of leadership
- Utilizing/analyzing editorials for expressions of leadership
- Team building and group projects
- Peer tutors

Other: _____
_____
_____

Math

Content Standards (Generalizations - Varies by District/State):

Number sense: fractions, decimals, percentages, exponents
Computations: addition, subtraction, multiplication, division
Shapes, properties, relationships (geometry)
Statistics and probability - data & graphs, mean, median, mode
Measurement: tools, formulas, similarity, trig, perimeter, area
Communication: language and symbols and terms
Problem solving: using problem solving strategies to solve problems
Math Power: Improving attitude, perseverance, & confidence

Leadership Opportunities within Math:

- Utilization of statistics for national problem solving by leaders
- Interpretation of statistics for positions presented
- Leaders in the mathematical world
- Application of math theories to every day decisions (decision making)
- Group dynamics and team building (group projects)
- Problem solving techniques
- Communication skills and presentation abilities
- Interpretation of historical significance of mathematical theories
- Connection between math and leadership styles and decisions
- Ethical beliefs and exponential impact of decisions
- Patience
- Peer tutors

Other: _____
_____
_____

Physical Education/Athletics

Content Standards (Generalizations - Varies by District/State):

Movement, body/space awareness
Individual skills and abilities
Participation in athletics for health-enhancement
Lifetime participation (life-sports)
Assessing, achieving, and maintaining fitness
Understanding benefits of physical activity - risk factors, safety, wellness
Contributions to healthy lifestyle - positive feelings, achievement, feeling of well-being, building relationships

Leadership Opportunities Within Physical Education:

- Team Building and group dynamics
- Fairness and benefiting others (e.g. team selections; including others)
- Communication skills
- Working with diverse populations
- Ethical decision making
- Role modeling
- Sportsmanship and humility
- Wellness and healthy lifestyles
- Appropriate confrontation and conflict resolution skills
- Peer tutors/role-models

Other: _____
_____
_____

Visual Arts*

Content Standards (Generalizations - Varies by District/State):

Recognize and use visual arts as form of communication
Interpreting and distinguishing meanings of visual images, themes, and ideas
Researching and using images, themes, and ideas to create art which reflect
 personal experiences
To know and apply elements of art, principles of design, and sensory and expressive
 features of visual arts
To know and apply visual arts materials, tools, techniques, and processes
To relate the visual arts to various historical and cultural traditions
Analyzing & evaluating the characteristics, merits, and meaning of works of art

Leadership Opportunities Within Physical Education:

- Resourcefulness
- Creative thinking
- Risk taking
- Communication skills using non-verbal expressions
- Group dynamics
- Tolerance and diversity
- Personal expression and "freedom of speech" discussions
- Understanding artistic expression of historical situations and dilemmas
- Ethics (funding the arts, NEA controversies, etc.)
- Forming and defending appropriate judgments
- Identifying and expressing standards
- Leaders in art
- Artistic expression as a means for meaningful dialogue among international leaders
- Peer tutors/role-models

Other: _____
_____
_____

*Other forms of art, both fine and practical have similar & relative content standards

Notes and Ideas

Sustaining Skills
Youth Leadership in the Community

Promoting youth leadership in the community is sometimes easier to do because there is less "territorialism" than with topics tied to curriculum. The opportunities created and encouraged in community youth programs should be approached with the same standards and clarity with which school-based curricular requirements are established. All programs typically have Mission Statements and Desired Outcomes identified in funding guides, training material, and promotional material. The next step is to add "content standards" for the programs serving youth. These content standards also can help teens link their experiences outside of school with their experiences in school. For drop-outs/stop-outs participating in community-based programs, promoting content standards may provide motivation to recognize the value of education and re-engage in school.

Service Learning/Volunteer Activities

Content Standards/Outcome Expectations (Examples):

- Youth will be sensitive to diverse populations and community needs
- Youth will learn tolerance and communication skills
- Youth will learn empathy
- Youth will recognize their role as an active member of the community
- Youth will learn to determine community priorities and needs
- Youth will learn to put words into action
- Youth will learn how to navigate funding programs and learn resourcefulness
- Youth will learn to lead others toward a common goal
- Youth will learn how to build allies and coalitions
- Youth will learn to identify their strengths and develop challenge areas

Boys/Girls/Youth Clubs

Content Standards/Outcome Expectations (Examples):

- Youth will be sensitive to diverse populations and community needs
- Youth will learn tolerance and communication skills
- Youth will learn empathy
- Youth will recognize their role as an active member of the community
- Youth will learn to determine community priorities and needs

- Youth will learn to put words into action
- Youth will learn how to navigate funding programs and learn resourcefulness
- Youth will learn to lead others toward a common goal
- Youth will learn how to build allies and coalitions

Probation/Diversion

Content Standards/Outcome Expectations (Examples):

- Youth will gain a greater understanding of their role in the community
- Youth will learn skills to help them set goals, maintain motivation, and recognize their importance as a contributing member of the community
- Youth will learn to make appropriate and positive choices in their lives
- Youth will learn tolerance and communication skills
- Youth will learn empathy
- Youth will learn to determine community priorities and needs
- Youth will learn how to access assistance and support in their community
- Youth will learn ethical decision making
- Youth will resolve their violation through reparative justice with their victim
- Youth will learn problem solving skills and decision making skills which do not entail violence
- Youth will learn how to make healthy choices
- Youth will learn how to take responsibility for choices and the implication of consequences
- Youth will have opportunities to develop a vision and goals for themselves

Adult Mentor (e.g. Big Bros/Big Sisters) Programs

Content Standards/Outcome Expectations (Examples):

- Youth will learn how to ask for help and learn about support systems in the community
- Youth will have appropriate role-models and mentors to rely upon
- Youth will learn alternatives for problem solving which do not include violence or lack of communication
- Youth will learn to tap into their strengths and improve on their challenge areas
- Youth will learn to lead others toward a common goal
- Youth will learn how to build allies and coalitions
- Youth will be sensitive to diverse populations and community needs

- Youth will learn tolerance and communication skills
- Youth will learn empathy
- Youth will recognize their role as an active member of the community
- Youth will learn to balance needs and wants and will learn skills to fulfill both
- Youth will learn to put words into action
- Youth will have opportunities to practice decision making, problem solving, and working with others while having guidance from a mentor

Teen Parent Programs

Content Standards/Outcome Expectations (Examples):

- Youth will learn role as a parent for developing children as leaders
- Youth will learn tolerance and communication skills
- Youth will learn empathy
- Youth will learn how to work with others to achieve a goal
- Youth will learn how to create personal vision and set goals
- Youth will learn to put words into action
- Youth will learn resourcefulness as a parent and a leader in their own lives and the lives of their children
- Youth will learn how to access help and support
- Youth will learn responsibility and follow-through
- Youth will learn how to build allies within the community
- Youth will learn patterns of role-modeling and appropriate conflict resolution skills

Anti-Violence Initiatives

Content Standards/Outcome Expectations (Examples):

- Youth will be sensitive to diverse populations and community needs
- Youth will learn tolerance and communication skills
- Youth will learn empathy
- Youth will recognize their role as an active member of the community
- Youth will learn to determine community priorities and needs
- Youth will learn to put words into action
- Youth will practice and learn appropriate conflict resolution skills
- Youth will learn how to make healthy choices

- Youth will learn how to take responsibility for choices and the implication of consequences
- Youth will learn to lead others toward a common goal
- Youth will learn how to build allies and coalitions
- Youth will learn how to seek help and assistance in times of need
- Youth will learn alternative for problem solving without violence
- Youth will learn resistance skills

Examples of Content Standards for Your Particular Program:

_____
_____
_____
_____
_____
_____
_____
_____
_____
_____
_____

What Activities/Efforts Currently Exist that Support Content Standards (either listed above or otherwise identified by your organization):

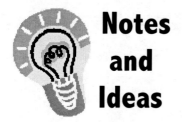
Notes and Ideas

Leadership in the "Real World"
(Relating leadership skills to the world of work)

General Workplace Competencies (Colorado Standards):
(Most states have similar guidelines)

Communication Skills: Demonstrates the ability to receive and relate information clearly and effectively

- Listening - receives, attends to, understands & responds to verbal & non-verbal messages
- Speaking - clearly organizes and effectively presents ideas orally
- Writing - organizes and effectively presents ideas and information in writing
- Interpreting - delineates & analyzes oral & written information; able to draw conclusions
- Negotiating - works toward agreement while maintaining position
- Persuading - communicates ideas to justify position, overcome resistance, & convince others

Organizational Skills: Demonstrates the ability to effectively and efficiently operate within a workplace

- Planning - devising and outlining a process to achieve a goal and timeline
- Time Mgt. - applies appropriate time to task and manages multiple priorities
- Using Resources - identifies, organizes, plans and allocates resources
- Systems Thinking - understands the nature of systems, develops & adapts systems to meet organizational needs
- Evaluating - collects, evaluates and uses data to monitor and improve performance

Thinking Skills: Demonstrates the ability to use reasoning

- Problem Solving - identifies and recognizes a problem, considers alternatives, devises and implements a logical plan of action
- Decision Making - uses a process to identify goals and constraints, evaluate alternatives and reach a conclusion
- Creative Thinking - generates new and innovative ideas
- Learning - uses efficient techniques to acquire and apply new knowledge and skills
- Analyzing - identifies bias of information sources, evaluates contradictory information and effectively manages information
- Mathematics - performs basic computations and solves practical problems by applying appropriate mathematical techniques

Worker Qualities: Demonstrates the characteristics of an effective worker

- Self-Management - demonstrates punctuality, readiness to work, initiative, and the capacity for life long learning and personal growth
- Team Member - contributes to group effort through cooperation and consensus
- Responsibility - follows through consistently with honesty and integrity
- Flexibility - shows versatility and the ability to change
- Leadership - creates a direction/vision for others to follow, aligns management methods with vision and implements a system of accountability
- Diversity - accepts differences and works well with individuals from a variety of backgrounds and/or divergent philosophies or ideas

Technology Skills: Demonstrates the ability to work with a variety of technologies and equipment

- Computer Literacy - demonstrates key boarding skills, uses computer programs and understands basic computer operations
- Selects Technology - choose appropriate procedures, tools or equipment
- Applies Technology - understands overall intent and proper procedures for using selected technology and equipment
- Uses Technology Information - interprets and uses data generated from a variety of technological devices

Integrated Leadership Education/Sustaining Skills
Determining Reasonable Outcomes

Examples of leadership behaviors which are DEVELOPMENTALLY reasonable to expect of Youth (level of competence will depend upon age and experiences):

- Project design and management, (youth may require adult structure, timelines, and assistance - work together to determine needs...avoid "just doing it" if youth get stuck)
- Project follow-through, master outlines, and delegating group responsibilities
- Confronting others on inappropriate behaviors (although they need to learn these skills first, as well as have them modeled consistently for them)
- Clearly knowing "right" from "wrong" behavior as a student leader
- Struggling with peer pressure but with guidance, encouragement, support and personal skill improvement can stand up for themselves against peer pressure
- Standing up for their beliefs among their peers. They may not stand up or share their beliefs with adult mentors unless invited to do so
- Organizing meetings, planning events, committees, etc.
- Appropriate behavior at mixed (adult/youth) events
- Developing public speaking skills (practice makes perfect...)
- Ability to mediate with peers
- Sensitivity to diverse populations and ability to demonstrate tolerance
- Developing anger management and conflict resolution skills
- Ability to differentiate between fact and opinion
- Reasonable standards for demonstrating responsibility, dependability, follow-through, etc. (These standards need to be developed with youth leaders and supported through modeling and establishing consequences for lack of follow-through)
- Fairly selecting members or leaders for projects, committees, organizations
- Setting and managing budgets for youth activities and projects
- Public relations design and appropriate promotion activities

- Fundraising and donation gathering
- Problem solving with group
- Public speaking and presentations
- Staff interviewing and selection
- Policy development, review, evaluation, modification, and adherence
- Facilitation of activities, leading discussion, debriefing and application of what is learned

Examples of ways to determine if your expectations are reasonable:

Ask ALL youth -

♦ What do you want to learn to become a better leader?
♦ In what situations is it difficult to be a leader?
♦ How can you get others to see you as a leader, especially if you have never been looked at like that before?
♦ What can I do to help you become a better leader?
♦ What can other teachers/staff/mentors, etc. do to help you?
♦ How can we work together as a school/organization to show everyone that leading and leadership are "cool"
♦ Where do you think adults in our school/organization could be more sensitive to your leadership talents and contributions?
♦ What is your perspective on this issue/topic/policy, etc.
♦ (After completing a project or presentation) Did you feel prepared to conduct that project (or activity)?
♦ In what ways could you have been better prepared?
♦ Do you feel that all youth in our program are given the chances to become leaders and to showcase their abilities?
♦ If people do not follow through with their responsibilities, what do you suggest we do?

Notes and Ideas

Integrated Leadership Education/Sustaining Skills
Methods for Assessing Youth Leadership Learning Outcomes

The process of "learning leadership" may pose challenges for individuals who are seeking statistical measurements of how to know a youth's leadership abilities have improved. Consequently, as we teach youth the value of "creative thinking" as leaders, it allows educators/instructors to model how creative thinking can provide methods for measuring learning.

Artwork/Drawing: Give youth opportunities to express themselves through art. Leadership topics can be understood in the form of a drawing or photograph. Give youth a large piece of paper, propose a leadership topic or issue, and allow them to express what it means to them. The metaphorical possibilities of drawing provide ample material for discussion and interpretation.

Attitudinal Surveys: You design them, youth fill them out. Or have youth design them and circulate to their peers. Use both box-checking and short essay/answer. Ask questions such as "how did you feel about leadership when we first started?" Move through progressive questions to find out if the learners have changed their feelings about leadership as well as asking questions specific to leadership skills/abilities they have learned/developed.

Commercials: Youth take their leadership subject matter and turn it into a commercial. It could be a written one (advertisement) for print media, a tape to be played on the radio, or a video. Have youth make it personal to their interests.

Community Projects: Youth can bring the results of work that they have done in the community. Or they can create a leadership project which will have a direct, positive, and measurable impact on their community. It could be social, ecological, or work done with a business.

Create a Story Board: Cartoonists pioneered the concept of story-boarding. Start with a sequence of roughly drawn pictures that capture each key moment. Put them up on a wall to create and trace the history of the project or the issue. This can be powerful with leadership issues such as ethical dilemmas, leadership project design, social issues facing youth, and communication topics.

Create a Wall-Size Mural: Have youth paint a mural representing leadership. There are endless topics which can be expressed and promoted in a mural.

Debates: These can come in many forms. A significant value of debates is in preparing for the actual debate! You may want to make your criteria for assessment very specific so that youth know how they will be appraised and you maintain the order of a true debate. Watching a professional debate between leaders (such as a political debate) can be a powerful discussion and learning tool as well.

Game Design: Youth know many games, most of them from their culture of growing up. Allow youth to take any game, such as Simon Says, Monopoly, Scrabble, Jeopardy, Trivial Pursuit, Wheel of Fortune, Concentration, Card Games, Ball games, etc. and redesign it related to leadership. For example, Scrabble can be played as instructed with the parameters that every word used must relate to leadership. Trivial Pursuit can be an excellent game, as is, for discussing/learning about leadership related topics (or people). Some games, played as instructed, also naturally lend themselves to discussions about leadership behaviors which emerge (such as Risk and Uno).

Interview: Leadership material/topics can be assessed if youth simply have time to talk freely about it. Casual, unstressful discussion/interview time is rarely used and yet, can be of great benefit. If youth will not get the chance to interview "real people," have youth formulate questions and extrapolate hypothetical answers. Even more powerful is when youth can interview existing leaders and interpret/present the results of that interview.

Journals/Learning Logs: For youth who are more private and introspective, you may learn much about what they learn (or know) through this reflective medium. Through journaling, the content becomes specific to learning and youth can create or answer questions about what and how they learned. They can also add their own feelings and possible applications of what they have learned.

Mind-Mapping: Let youth create huge, poster-sized maps of what they know about leadership or leadership topics. These webbed, thematic graphic organizers offer colorful, peripheral thoughts organized around a key idea. They were popularized by Tony Buzan, Michael Gelb, and Nancy Margulies. Mind Maps provide an excellent vehicle for understanding relationships, themes and associations of ideas.

Model Making: In some cased, youth can build a scaled-down or working -size model of the material. This can be particularly useful in demonstrating their understanding of the material when it is physical and involves steps or processes.

Montage/Collage: This format provides a vehicle for collecting and assembling thoughts and ideas. It's actually a combination between a mind-map, a sculpture, and a drawing! The more choice and freedom you offer your youth, the more likely you are to get something really innovative. A technology equivalent is a web page design!

Multi-Media: Youth can make a video, cassette tape, CD, or web-site related to leadership. Insist that it be quality and help provide access to the necessary resources. Your rubric will help you and your students evaluate these "subjective" mediums.

Music: Most leadership material/issues can be set to music, written about in music, or performed as music. Lyrics of existing songs can also be used to help youth understand how they learn leadership. Or they may rewrite an existing song to emphasize leadership issues.

Newspaper Articles: Let youth create their own mock-up front page of a leadership topic. They take many points of view and each has to be related to their own life. That way it could be covered from personal, financial, sociological, historical, literary, mathematical, physical, or scientific aspects.

Performance: Let youth do drama or theater on the material. Some leadership topics lend themselves to be performed (e.g. social issues, controversial topics, role modeling, etc.). Allow youth time to do a quality job preparing or writing their script. Then create a fun stage for them to perform upon.

Personal Goals Checklist: Youth set original learning goals, interim goals, and revise them as time goes on. Goals are self-assessed (or monitored by an adult "partner"): if the goal is reached, when the goal is reached, how it was reached, and appropriate reassessment. Each youth shares this analysis with the adult partner.

Plan and Produce a Mini-Conference: Youth plan an "experts" gathering on leadership. They gather speakers, plan the talks/workshops, organize the logistics, put it on, and evaluate it. Can either be just planned or actually carried out. The best learning situations are workshops/conferences which are actually conducted. This assessment is a significant one and should not be used half-heartedly!

Sculpture: Similar to other art mediums, leadership learning can be represented as a physical object or sculpture. In addition, existing sculptures or objects can be used to prompt youth to discuss the issues surrounding the piece or what leadership issues are evoked by looking at the object.

Student Teaching: Provide youth time to think the subject out first, then make their own notes or create mind-maps on the subject. The more props, music and visual aides used, the more meaningful the presentation will be. Provide a "pre-student teaching" lesson on different learning styles/modalities in order to assist them with this experiential learning opportunity. Keep the experience fun by providing students with choice on their leadership topic and promoting low-risk peer support. Give each youth (or team of youths) time to teach their topic to the class.

Student/Youth Written Tests: Let students figure out what's important and what's not. Ask them to create their own test...you can set some basic criteria and still keep plenty of room for creativity.

Notes and Ideas

Integrated Leadership Education/Sustaining Skills
Activities That Promote Youth Leadership Development

- Academic Experiences (Leadership Across the Curriculum)
- Athletics (Team or Individual; School or Community)
- Baby-sitting
- Band or other Musical activities
- Cheer Leading or Spirit Teams
- Church Youth Groups/Youth Ministry
- Coaching (younger students, Pee-Wee leagues)
- Community Advisory Boards (Parks & Rec., Churches, Non-Profit agencies, etc.)
- Cultural organizations and traditions
- Debate/Youth Toastmasters
- Environmental activities (Outward Bound, Sierra Club, Outdoor Volunteer Clubs)
- Family Activities
- Fine and Practical Art activities (emphasizing the youth's abilities)
- Girl Scouts/Boy Scouts
- Intergenerational Experiences (e.g. Adopt-A-Grandparent)
- Internships (Related to future goals)
- Newspaper (writing for school or in the community)
- Parenting/Child Development (either classes or personal experience)
- Peer Mediation/Intervention Programs
- School Advisory Boards/Community & Youth Boards
- School and Community Clubs or Organizations (4-H, Future Farmers, Key Club, Interact, Young Life, Language Clubs, Academic Clubs, Honor Society, Vocational Clubs, etc.)
- School Council/School Government/Youth Board
- Student Assisting (office aid, teacher's aid, etc.)
- Student/Youth Identified Projects (e.g. School improvement projects, School/Community pride, Service projects, etc.)
- Theater or Drama Activities
- Tutoring (Same age/Younger age)
- Volunteer/Community Service Activities
- Work
- Youth Representatives on City/Town Commissions

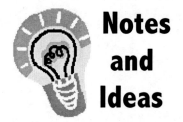
Notes and Ideas

Developing Your Skill as a Leadership Educator

- Read up on leadership theories, attitudes, and trends
- Talk with youth leaders around your school and community
- Observe youth leaders in action
- Teach a leadership class - just like youth, adults do learn best through hands on experience!
- Participate in a Ropes Course
- Take a training class on facilitating a Ropes Course
- Attend a lecture or presentation given by a business leader or other individual who is recognized for leadership skills - learn to translate what you learn into the classroom and with a younger population
- Volunteer in the community - many service experiences are excellent opportunities to develop your own leadership skills
- Develop an evaluation form of your skills which your students can complete and give back to you (allow for anonymity...you get better feedback!)
- Participate in the school improvement process; volunteer to chair a committee or lead some other group process
- Read everything you can on leadership in current events (in the newspaper, periodicals, etc.). Learn to read material with an eye for what leadership behaviors are developed or addressed (such as ethics, creative thinking, problem solving, communication, appropriate conflict resolution, etc.)
- Co-plan and co-teach with a student leader, a class session on a leadership topic. Take time after the experience to discuss successes and challenges
- Attend professional development trainings on leadership topics
- Co-teach with teachers in various academic disciplines a class session on leadership (or a leadership class)
- Coach a youth athletic team
- Sponsor a school club or other youth activity
- Serve as detention monitor one day and instead of having the youth do "clean-up", design a leadership lesson (related to why they are in detention) and have them participate in it during the time. Leadership lessons DO apply to truancy and misbehavior!
- Find a mentor and use that person to help you improve your skills as a leadership educator
- Take a college course on Organizational Behavior, Leadership Styles, etc. (most of the colleges/universities all over offer many)
- Watch and discuss movies as they related to leadership (many movies do!)
- Practice, practice, practice

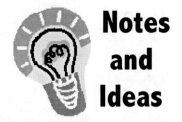# Notes and Ideas

Final Thoughts...
What Adult Mentors can do to Promote the Development of Leadership Skills & Abilities

- Work with youth to define "Leadership" and "Leader"
- Post the definition in a prominent place for the youth you serve
- Identify the leadership characteristics you desire youth in your program to possess and create learning opportunities around these characteristics... volunteer at a shelter (empathy & tolerance), participate in a community forum (community leadership), register to vote and explain the voting process (modeling the way & political leadership), attend a cultural event from a culture different than your own (tolerance & diversity), practice ethical decisions (ethics, values & decision making), etc.
- Communicate (don't just "talk") with youth...if you don't know how, attend professional development classes or buy one of the many books on communicating with youth (generally found in parenting departments of bookstores)
- Value the perspective of youth in your program/school
- Value the current experiences of youth in your program/school
- When youth in your program/school make a mistake, calmly talk about what they learned from the experience and how they can use what they learned. In other words, allow for mistakes, process through them, and apply the learning
- Avoid living vicariously! Let them lead!
- Explore ways that youth can learn new things and apply what they have learned...as with other things, learning leadership takes practice. Talk about experiences along the way
- Make "leadership" and "becoming a leader" a part of daily conversation school, and family activities. Base this on the definition that you and the youth determined. Include youth leadership tips and youth leadership recognitions in your newsletter
- Relate leadership to all activities
- Identify what is important to the youth in your program and find ways to create leadership opportunities around those topics/issues
- Learn and practice appropriate conflict resolution with youth
- Set standards for demonstrating leadership abilities
- Consistently recognize leadership accomplishments
- Be attentive to "teachable leadership moments"
- Listen and be patient...developing leaders is an ongoing process
- Be supportive and encouraging
- MODEL WHAT YOU EXPECT

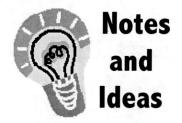

Notes and Ideas

Final Thoughts
Inspiring Youth Leaders

- Be truthful
- Encourage differences
- Be trusting and trustworthy
- Promote challenges and high standards
- Look for the diamond in the rough
- Expose them to opportunities - no matter what!
- Be non-judgmental
- Believe in them wholeheartedly
- Allow for mistakes
- Confront Perfectionism
- Model the way
- Recognize fear and concern from them that they won't be taken seriously
- Offer autonomy and allow it to be earned and maintained
- Accept their weaknesses and promote their strengths
- Redefine success and failure
- Redesign your attitude (Seek feedback/perspectives from youth you serve)
- Celebrate accomplishments
- Create attainable visions
- Listen closely
- Question yourself
- Relinquish Power in your classroom
- Allow the students to be the experts
- Provide ample chances to practice leadership
- Advocate for their ideas and promote their triumphs
- Humility, Humor, Hopefulness
- Spread the word
- Relate to their reality
- Be creative & innovative
- Give Respect - Earn Respect
- Patience
- Continue to add to your knowledge of the subject - constantly explore and investigate leadership topics and experiences for yourself and youth

Leadership Program Action Plan

My first goal of our youth leadership program is:

_____
_____
_____

The first action I will take to achieve this goal is:

_____
_____
_____

The people who will help or support me are:

_____ _____ _____

The things or people which (who) may get in my way are:

_____ _____ _____

I will be ready to deal with these things by:

_____
_____
_____

I will know I have achieved this goal when:

_____
_____

I will check my progress on the following dates:

_____ _____ _____

This goal will be accomplished by the following date: _____

Notes and Ideas

Bibliography & Resources

Bibliography (Suggested resources/readings)

Leadership Library

101 Ways to Integrate Personal Development Into Core Curriculum: Lessons in Character Education for Grades K-12
Mary Ann Conroy. University Press of America, 2000.

A Higher Standard of Leadership: Lessons from the Life of Gandhi
By Keshavan Nair. Berrett-Koehler, 1994.

A Social Change Model of Leadership: Guidebook, Version III.
Higher Education Research Institute, University of California, Los Angeles, 1996. [Order through National Clearinghouse for Leadership Programs - http://www.nclp.umd.edu]

A Whack on the Side of the Head: How to Unlock Your Mind for Innovation
Roger von Oech. Warner, 1983.

Bottomless Baggie
Karl Rohnke. Kendall/Hunt, 1991.

Bridges to Accessibility: A Primer for Including Persons with Disabilities in Adventure Curricula
Mark D. Havens. Kendall/Hunt, 1992.

Building Everyday Leadership in All Teens (Curriculum guide for teachers and youth workers) Accompanying student workbook available, see **Everyday Leadership**
Mariam G. MacGregor. Free Spirit Publishing, 2007.

Cowstails and Cobras II: A Guide to Games, Initiatives, Ropes Course, and Adventure Curriculum
Karl Rohnke. Kendall/Hunt, 1989.

Cradle of Greatness: What Our Eight Greatest Presidents had in Common in Youth
Donald G. Ferguson. 1st Books Library, 2001.

Credibility: How Leaders Gain and Lose It, Why People Demand It
James Kouzes and Barry Posner. Jossey-Bass, 1993.

Designing Student Leadership Programs: Transforming the Leadership Potential of Youth
Mariam G. MacGregor. Youthleadership.com, 3rd Edition, 2005.

Developing Student Leaders: How to Motivate, Select, Train, Empower Your Kids to Make a Difference (Youth Ministry)
Ray Johnstone. Youth Specialties, Zondervan Publishing House, 1992.

Directory of American Youth Organizations: A guide to 500 Clubs, Groups, Troops, Teams, Societies, Lodges, and More for Young People
Judith B. Erickson. Free Spirit Publishing, 1998.

Encouraging the Heart: A Leader's Guide to Rewarding and Recognizing Others
James M. Kouzes & Barry Z. Posner. Jossey-Bass, 1999

Everyday Leadership: Attitudes and Actions for Respect and Success (Teen Guidebook)
Mariam G. MacGregor. Free Spirit Publishing, 2007.

Games Trainers Play: Experiential Learning Exercises
Edward E. Scannell & John Newstrom. McGraw-Hill, 1980.

Girls and Young Women Leading the Way: 20 True Stories about Leadership
Frances A. Karnes and Suzanne M. Bean. Free Spirit Publishing, 1993.

In Search of Excellence: Lessons from America's Best-run Companies
Tom Peters. Warner Books, 1988.

Kick It In! Developing the Self-Motivation to Take the Lead
Fran Kick, 2001.

Lead Now or Step Aside: The Ultimate Handbook for Student Leaders
Eric Chester, Editor. ChesPress, 2000.

Leaders: The Strategies for Taking Charge
Warren Bennis and Burt Nanus. Harperbusiness, 1997.

Leadership
James MacGregor Burns. Harper Collins, 1985.

The Leadership Challenge Planner: An Action Guide to Achieving Your Personal Best
James M. Kouzes & Barry Z. Posner. Josey-Bass, 1999.

Leadership Education: A Source Book of Courses and Programs
Frank H. Freeman, Mary K. Schwartz, Kristin P. Axtman
Center for Creative Leadership, 1998.

Leadership Lessons: Lessons to Lead By
National Association of Secondary School Principals, 1998.

Lead, Follow, or Get Out of the Way
Jim Lundy. Berkley Books, 1986.

Leadership in the Movies (DVD)
Motivational Media Assemblies/Herff-Jones. 2003.

Leadership is an Art
Max DePree. Doubleday, 1989.

Leadership Jazz
Max DePree. Dell, 1993.

Leadership Resources: A Guide to Training and Development Tools (8th Edition)
Frank H. Freeman, Mary K. Schwartz, Kristin P. Axtman
Center for Creative Leadership, 2000.

Let's Talk! Leadership For Kids: Questions to Get Things Started (other format)
Mariam MacGregor. Youthleadership.com, 2005.

Making Common Sense: Leadership As Meaning-Making in a Community of Practice
William H. Drath & Charles J. Palus. Center for Creative Leadership, Greensboro, NC, 1994.

Managing With Carrots
Adrian Gostick and Chester Elton. Gibbs-Smith Publishing, 2001.

More Games Trainers Play: Experiential Learning Exercises
Edward E. Scannell & John Newstrom. McGraw-Hill, 1983.

More Leadership Lessons: 50 Lesson Plans for Teaching Leadership Concepts and Skills.
National Association of Secondary School Principals, 2003.

More New Games...and Playful Ideas from the New Games Foundation
Andrew Fluegelman. Dolphin/Doubleday, 1981.

Nurturing the Leader within Your Child: What Every Parent Needs to Know
Tim Elmore. Thomas Nelson Publishers, 2001.

On Becoming A Leader: The Leadership Classic--Updated And Expanded
William Bennis. Perseus Publishing, Revised Edition, 2003.

Principle-Centered Leadership
Steven Covey. Summit Books, 1991.

Pigeonholed in the Land of Penguins: A Tale of Seeing Beyond Stereotypes
Barbara "BJ" Hateley & Warren H. Schmidt. American Management Association, 2000

Politics, Leadership, and Justice
The Great Books Foundation (50th Anniversary Series), 1998.

Race Matters
Cornel West. Beacon Press, 1993.

Setting Your Genius Free: How to Discover your Spirit and Calling
Dick Richards. Berkley Books, 1998.

Shackleton's Way: Leadership Lessons from the Great Antarctic Explorer
By Margot Morrell and Stephanie Capparell. Viking Publishing, 2001.

Silver Bullets: A Guide to Initiative Problems, Adventure Games & Trust Activities
Karl Rohnke. Kendall/Hunt, 1994.

Six Thinking Hats
Edward DeBono. Little, Brown, and Company, 1985.

Stand Up and Be Counted: The Volunteer Resource Book
J. Knipe. Simon & Schuster, 1992.

Still More Games Trainers Play: Experiential Learning Exercises
Edward E. Scannell & John Newstrom. McGraw-Hill, 1991.

Students Taking the Lead: The Challenges and Rewards of Empowering Youth in Schools
Judith A. Boccia (Editor). Jossey-Bass, 1997.

Take Action! A Guide to Active Citizenship
Marc Kielburger and Craig Kielburger. John Wiley & Sons, 2002.

Teambuilding with Teens: Activities for Leadership, Decision-Making, and Group Success
Mariam G. MacGregor. Free Spirit Publishing, 2008.

Teens Can Make It Happen: Nine Steps for Success
Stedman Graham. Fireside, 2000.

The 7 Habits of Highly Effective Teens
Sean Covey. Fireside, 1998.

The Book of Virtues: A Treasury of Great Moral Stories
William J. Bennett. Touchstone (Simon & Schuster), 1993.

The Bottomless Bag
Karl Rohnke. Kendall/Hunt, 1991.

The Complete Guide to Service Learning: Proven, Practical Ways to Engage Students in Civic Responsibility, Academic Curriculum & Social Action
Catheryn Berger Kaye. Free Spirit Publishing, 2004.

The Complete Idiot's Guide to Leadership
Andrew J. DuBrin. Alpha Books (division of MacMillan), 1998.

The Encyclopedia of Icebreakers: Structured Activities that Warm Up, Motivate, Challenge, Acquaint and Energize
Susan Forbess-Green. Pfeiffer & Company, 1980.

The Encyclopedia of Team-Building Activities
J. William Pfeiffer, ed. Pfeiffer & Company, 1990.

The Fifth Discipline: The Art and Practice of the Learning Organization
Peter Senge. Doubleday Publishing, 1990.

The Leadership Challenge: How 3rd Edition
James Kouzes and Barry Posner. Jossey-Bass, 2003.

The Moral Compass: Stories for Life's Journey
William J. Bennett. Simon & Schuster, 1995.

The New Leaders: Guidelines on Leadership Diversity in America.
Ann M. Morrison. Jossey-Bass, 1992.

The Pursuit of Wow: Every Person's Guide to Topsy Turvy Times
Tom Peters. Vintage Books, 1994.

The Tipping Point: How Little Things Can Make a Big Difference
Malcolm Gladwell. Little, Brown and Company, 2000; 2002.

Tricks for Trainers
Dave Arch. Resources for Organizations, Inc., 1993.

Wake Up Your Creative Genius
Kurt Hanks and Jay Parry. Crisp Publishers, 1991.

Women of Influence, Women of Change: A Cross-Generational Study of Leaders and Social Change
Helen Astin and Carol Leland. Jossey-Bass, Inc. 1991.

Youth Leadership: A Guide to Understanding Leadership Development in Adolescents
Josephine A. van Linden & Carl I. Fertman. Jossey-Bass, 1998.

Youth Leadership in Action: A Guide to Cooperative Games & Group Activities, Written By and For Youth Leaders
Project Adventure. Kendall/Hunt, 1994.

Youth Leadership In Action (Instructor Manual and Youth Workbook) [Various ages- Elementary, Middle, High School]
The J.W. Fanning Institute for Leadership http://www.fanning.uga.edu

Visit http://www.youthleadership.com for updates to this list.

Journals/Magazines/Publishers

Crisp Publishers, Inc. (Various titles on leadership topics)
1200 Hamilton Court
Menlo Park, CA 94025
http://www.crisp-pub.com/

Fast Company
Subscription Information: P.O. Box 52764
Boulder, CO 80323-2764
888-237-2071
http://www.fastcompany.com

Jossey-Bass Publishers, Inc. (Various titles on leadership topics)
350 Sansome Street
San Francisco, CA 94104-1304
800-956-7739
http://www.josseybass.com

Journal of College & Character
Center for The Study of Values in College Student Development
College of Educational Leadership and Policy Studies
113 Stone Building
Florida State University
Tallahassee, FL 32306-4452
850.644.6446
email: HardeeC@coe.fsu.edu
http://www.collegevalues.org

The Journal of Leadership and Organizational Studies
Subscription Information:
1050 West Bristol Road
Flint, MI 48507
1.800.469.3165 or 810.766.4390
https://www.baker.edu/departments/leadership/jls-main.cfm

Leadership for Student Activities (magazine)
NASSP Department of Student Activities
1904 Association Drive
Reston, VA 20191-1537
703.860.0200
email: leadershipmag@principals.org
http://www.nasc.us/s_nasc/sec.asp?CID=162&DID=5354

Leadership Review
Kravis Leadership Institute
Claremont McKenna College
850 Columbia Avenue
Claremont, CA 91711
909.607.9332
email: leadership.review@claremontmckenna.edu
http://www.leadershipreview.org

Student Leader Magazine
Subscription Information:
888-547-6310
http://www.studentleader.com

Youth Today: The Newspaper on Youth Work
Subscription Information:
1200 17th Street, NW 4th Floor
Washington, DC 20036
202.785.0764
http://www.youthtoday.org

Visit http://www.youthleadership.com for updates to this list.

Organizations/Websites

AM Horizons Training Group
7951 Greenwood Dr.
Mounds View, MN 55112
351.387.1866
email: AMNeok@aol.com
http://www.amhorizons.com

American Student Government Association (ASGA)
P.O. Box 14081
Gainesville, FL 32604-2081
877.275.2742
email: info@asgaonline.com
http://www.asgaonline.com

Arizona Collegiate Leadership Conference
Center for Student Involvement & Leadership
University of Arizona
Tucson, AZ 85721-0017
520.626.1572
email: aclc@email.arizona.edu
http://www.union.arizona.edu/csil/aclc/

Association of Leadership Educators
(address varies based upon current year Executive Committee members)
www.aces.uiuc.edu/~ALE/

Bruderhof Saving Childhood Forum
The Bruderhof Foundation, Inc.
2032 Route 213 / PO Box 903
Rifton, New York 12471
845.658.8351
email: tbf@bruderhof.com
http://www.savingchildhood.org

Building Partnerships with Youth
National 4-H Council and the University of Arizona
PO Box 210033
Tucson, AZ 85721-0033
520.621.3399
http://msg.calsnet.arizona.edu/fcs/index.cfm

CampFire USA Headquarters
4601 Madison Avenue
Kansas City, MO 64112
816.756.1950
email: info@campfireusa.org
http://www.camfireusa.org/teens

Campus Compact
Brown University
Box 1975
Providence, RI 02912
401.863.1119
email: campus@compact.org
http://www.compact.org

Canadian Association of Student Activity Advisors (CASAA)
email: casaa@golden.net
http://www.casaa-resources.net

CCD Training
6006 Holly Crest
Sachse, Texas 75048
972.442.8235
email: kyleandcrystal@verizon.net
http://www.ccdtraining.com

Center for Creative Leadership
P.O. Box 26300
Greensboro, NC 27438-6300
336.545.2810
email: info@leaders.ccl.org
http://www.ccl.org

Center for Ethical Leadership
1401 E. Jefferson, Suite 505
Seattle, WA 98122
206.328.3020
http://www.ethicalleadership.org

Character Counts! National Office
The Josephson Institute
4640 Admiralty Way #1001
Marino del Rey, CA 90292
email: info@jiethics.org
http://www.charactercounts.org
http://www.josephsoninstitute.org

Congressional Youth Leadership Council
Includes:
- National Young Leaders Conference
- Global Young Leaders Conference
- Junior National Young Leaders Conference
- National Young Leaders State Conference
- Presidential Youth Inaugural Conference
- Junior Presidential Youth Inaugural Conference
- Global Young Leader's Summit

1110 Vermont Avenue, NW, Suite 320
Washington, DC 20005
202.638.0008
email: cylc@cylc.org
http://www.cylc.org

Community Partnerships with Youth, Inc.
6744 Falcon Ridge Court
Indianapolis, IN 46278
317.875.5756
email: thejourneyemail@aol.com
www.cpyinc.org

The Community Leadership Association
200 S. Meridian Street, Suite 250
Indianapolis, IN 46225
800.553.2337
email: info@communityleadership.org
www.communityleadership.org

Dick Richards Workshops and Coaching
"Is Your Genius At Work"
13041 S 42nd Place
Phoenix, AZ 85044
480.753.0131
email: dickrichards@ongenius.com
http://www.ongenius.com
http://www.ongenius.com/blog

Envision EMI
1919 Gallows Road, Suite 700
Vienna, VA 22182
703.584.9324
email: envision@envisionemi.com
http://www.envisionemi.com

EnVision Leadership
145 Hanover St.
Boston, MA 02108
Tel: 617-266-2502
Fax: 617-266-8185
team@envisionleadership.com
www.envisionleadership.com

Emergingleader.com
P.O. Box 360434
Columbus, OH 43236
email: info@emergingleader.com
http://www.emergingleader.com

Experience Based Learning, Inc.
Experience Based Adventures, Inc.
6260 E. Riverside Boulevard, #104
Rockford, IL 61111
815.637.2969
eba@e-b-a.org
http://www.ebl.org
http://www.e-b-a.org

FuturePoint
287 East Oakland Park Blvd
Ft. Lauderdale, FL 33334
954.564.0555
email: keith@futurepoint.org
http://www.futurepoint.org

Gardner Carney Leadership Institute
Fountain Valley School of Colorado
6155 Fountain Valley School Road
Colorado Springs, CO 80911
719.390.7035 x233
email: gcli@fvs.edu
http://www.fvs.edu/gcli/default.asp

Growing Leaders
5315 Lexington Woods Lane
Alpharetta, GA 30005
email: info@growingleaders.com
http://www.growingleaders.com

G.U.T.S. "Guys & Gals Utilizing Their Strengths"
7816 Williams Moyers Avenue
Albuquerque, NM 87122
505.797.0961
email: questions@presentation-style.com
http://www.presentation-style.com/guts

Higher Education Research Institute
(Social Change Model of Leadership)
University of California, Los Angeles
3005 Moore Hall Box 951521
Los Angeles, CA 90095-1521
310.825.1925
HERI@ucla.edu
http://www.gseis.ucla.edu/heri/heri.html

Hugh O'Brian Youth Leadership (HOBY)
(Chapters nationwide)
10880 Wilshire Boulevard, Suite 2121
Los Angeles, CA 90024
310.474.4370
http://www.hoby.org/

The Jepson School of Leadership @ the University of Richmond
28 Westhampton Way
Richmond, VA 23173
804.289.8008
http://www.richmond.edu/academics/leadership/

Josh Shipp Productions
3309 Beverly Drive
Edmond, OK 73013
877.582.6896
email: Josh@JoshShipp.com
http://www.joshshipp.com

J.W. Fanning Institute for Leadership
University of Georgia
1234 Lumpkin Street
Athens, Georgia 30602-3552
706-542-2830
FAX 706-542-7007
http://www.fanning.uga.edu

Just For Youth, Inc.
6400 Baltimore National Pike
Suite 173
Baltimore, MD 21228
443.768.4108
email: justforyouthinc@yahoo.com
http://www.just4youth.net

Kick It In!
441 Maple Springs Drive
Centerville, OH 45458-9232
937.439.2698
http://www.kickitin.com

KIDS Consortium (service-learning)
215 Lisbon Street, Suite 12
Lewiston, Maine 04240
207.784.0956
emaill: kap@kidsconsortium.org
http://www.kidsconsortium.org

The Leadership Challenge
c/o Jossey-Bass
350 Sansome Street
San Francisco, CA 94501
800.956.7739
http://www.theleadershipchallenge.com

The Leading Edge @ High Mountain Institute
PO Box 970
Leadville, CO 80461
ph: 719.486.8200
email: kbartlett@hminet.org
http://www.hminet.org/page.php?pname=edge

Leadership Education for Asian Pacifics, Inc. (LEAP, Inc.)
327 East Second Street, Suite 226
Los Angeles, CA 90012
213.485.1422
email: leap@leap.org
http://www.leap.org

Leadership Village
314 Carol Lane
Elyria, OH 44035
440.329.5333
email: info@LeadershipVillage.com
http://www.LeadershipVillage.com

Leaders Today
50 High Oak Trail
Richmond Hill, Ontario
Canada L4E 3L9
905.889.9739
email: training101@hotmail.com
http://www.leaderstoday.com

L.I.T. (Leader in Training) Experience
316 Victoria Street East Box 823
Dudalk Ont
N0C 1B0
519.923.5983
email: litexperience@hotmail.com
http://www.litexperience.com

Macheo Payne Youth Leadership & Development
150 Frank Ogawa Plaza, Suite 4211
Oakland, CA 94612
510.238.6333
email: mpayne@macheopayne.com
http://www.macheopayne.com

Mid-Atlantic Programs/Hurricane Island Outward Bound School
3250 West Sedgeley Drive
East Fairmount Park
Philadelphia, PA 19130
215.232.9130 (Philadelphia)   410.448.1721 (Baltimore)
email: philadelphia@hurricanheisland.org
email: baltimore@hurricaneisland.org
http://www.hurricaneisland.org

National Association of Elementary School Principals (NAESP)
1615 Duke Street
Alexandria, VA 22314
800.386.2377
email: naesp@naesp.org
http://www.naesp.org

National Association of Secondary School Principals (NASSP)
National Association of Student Councils (NASC)
1904 Association Drive
Reston, VA 20191-1537
703.860.0200
800.253.7746
email: dsa@principals.org
http://www.nasc.us/s_nasc/index.asp

National Center on Secondary Education and Transition
Institute on Community Integration
University of Minnesota, 6 Pattee Hall
150 Pillsbury Drive SE
Minneapolis MN 55455
612.624.2097
email: ncset@umn.edu
http://www.ncset.org

National Clearinghouse for Leadership Programs (NCLP)
1135 Stamp Union
University of Maryland
College Park, MD 20742-7174
301.405.0799
http://www.nclp.umd.edu/

National Clearinghouse on Families & Youth
P.O. Box 13505
Silver Spring, MD 20911-3505
301.608.8098
email: info@ncfy.com
http://www.ncfy.com

National League of Cities
Institute for Youth, Education, and Families
1301 Penn Avenue NW
Washington, DC 20004-1763
202.626.3000
http://www.nlc.org/nlc_org/site/programs/institute_for_youth_education_and_families/index.cfm

National Resource Center for Youth Services (NRCYS)
4502 E. 41st Street, Building 4W
Tulsa, OK 74135-2512
918.660.3700
http://www.nrcys.ou.edu

National Society for Experiential Education
3509 Haworth Drive
Suite 257
Raleigh, NC 27009
http://www.nsee.org/

National Student Leadership Conference
Office of Admissions
111 West Jackson Boulevard, 7th Floor
Chicago, IL 60604
800.994.6752 (in continental US)
312.322.9999 (outside continental US)
email: info@NSLCleaders.org
http://www.nslcleaders.org
http://www.nslcinfo.org

National Teen Leadership Program (NTLP)
738 Commons Drive
Sacramento, CA 95825
800.550.1950
email: info@teenleader.org
www.teenleader.org

National Youth Leadership Council (NYLC)
1910 W. County Road B
St. Paul, MN 55113
651.631.3672
nylcinfo@nylc.org
http://www.nylc.org

National Youth Leadership Forum
Includes:
- National Youth Leadership Forum on Defense, Intelligence and Diplomacy (202.777.4002)
- National Youth Leadership Forum on Law (202.777.4003)
- National Youth Leadership Forum on Medicine (202.628.6090)
- National Youth Leadership Forum on Technology (202.777.4100)
- National Youth Leadership Forum on Nursing (202.777.0581)

1110 Vermont Avenue, N.W., Suite 330
Washington, DC 20005
email: info@nylf.org
http://www.nylf.org

Outward Bound (Locations World-Wide)
Outward Bound-USA National Office
Route 9D - R2 Box 280
Garrison, NY 10524-9757
800.243.8520
914.424.4000
http://www.outwardbound.org

Path of Success, Inc.
Choate Rosemary Hall
333 Christian Street
Wallingford, CT 06492
877.898.7284
email: psa@pathofsuccess.org
http://www.pathofsuccess.org

PeaceJam
P.O. Box 480705
Denver, CO 80248-0705
303.455.2099
http://www.peacejam.org

Pelletier Homes for Youth
106 Wallace Avenue,
Toronto, Ontario, M6H 1T5
416.534.7309
email: info@pelletierhomes.org
http://www.pelletierhomes.org

Points of Light Youth Leadership Institute
Points of Light Foundation
1400 I ("Eye") Street, NW, Suite 800
Washington, DC 20005
202-729-8000
email: Info@PointsofLight.org
http://www.pyli.org/

Project Adventure (4 offices nationwide)
http://www.pa.org/

Resilience In Action
PO Box 90319 San Diego,
CA 92169-2319
ph: 858.488.5034
email: nhenderson@resiliency.com
http://www.resiliency.com

Resilience Partners
230 South 500 East, Suite 100
Salt Lake City, Utah 84102
801. 532.1484
email: info@samgoldstein.com
email: contact@drrobertbrooks.com
http://www.raisingresilientkids.com

Rocky Mountain Institute for Leadership Advancement
524 Emery Street
Longmont, CO 80501
303.684.6480
888.709.0088
email: info@rmleadership.com
http://www.rmleadership.com

Santa Clara University - Center for Student Leadership
Benson Center
500 El Camino Real
Santa Clara, CA 95050
408.554.4745
http://www.scu.edu/csl

Sierra Club (Inner City Outings)
85 Second Street, 2nd Floor
San Francisco, CA 94105
415.977.5500
http://www.sierraclub.org/chapters/pa/pinchot/innercity.html
(or contact local Sierra Club office)

Simulation Training Systems
P.O. Box 910
Del Mar, CA 92014
800.942.2900
email: sts2@cts.com
http://www.stsintl.com

Publisher of "Star Power" "BaFa BaFa" and other simulation activities

Think Like A Genius, LLC
4950 S. Yosemite Street,
Suite F2-325
Greenwood Village, CO 80111
303.649.9388
email: tsiler@thinklikeagenius.com
http://www.thinklikeagenius.com/highband/index.html

United National Indian Tribal Youth, Inc. (UNITY)
P.O. Box 25042
Oklahoma City, OK 73125
405.236.2800
email: unity@unityinc.org
http://www.unityinc.org

Vision XY , Inc.
P. O. Box 1702
El Cerrito, CA 94530
954.791.7991
email: visionxy@visionxy.com
http://www.visionxy.com/index.html

Volunteer Toronto
416.961.6888
http://www.volunteertoronto.on.ca/yintro.asp

What Kids Can Do, Inc.
P.O. Box 603252
Providence, RI 02906
401.247.7665
email: info@whatkidscando.org
http://www.whatkidscando.org

Youth Activism Project
Wendy Lesko
Executive Director
PO Box E
Kensington MD 20895
800.KID.POWER
email: info@youthactivism.com
http://www.youthactivism.com

Youth on Board
58 Day Street, 3rd Floor
P.O. Box 440322
Somerville, MA 02144
617.623.9900 x 1242
email: YouthonBoard@aol.com
http://www.youthonboard.org

Youth Leadership Initiative
University of Virginia Center for Politics
2400 Old Ivy Road
P.O. Box 400806
Charlottesville, VA 22904
866.514.8389
email: ylihelp@virginia.edu
http://www.youthleadership.net

Youth Leadership Program of Oakland Unified School District
121 East 11th Street
Oakland, CA 94606
510-879-8382
email: mlevine@ousd.k12.ca.us

Youth Leadership for Vital Communities Initiative
c/o Center for 4-H Youth Development
270 B McNamara Alumni Center
200 Oak Street SE
Minneapolis, MN 55455
612.624.7988
email: moenx010@umn.edu
http://www.ylvc.org

YouthLink (Global Youth Action Network)
Foundation of America
3020 Children's Way, MC #5093
San Diego, CA 92123
619.576.4044
http://www.youthlink.org

YouthNOISE
2000 M Street, NW, Suite 500
Washington, DC 20036
or
YouthNOISE
1255 Post Street
Suite 1120
San Francisco, CA 94109
email: help@youthnoise.com
email: support@youthnoise.com
http://www.youthnoise.com

YouthVenture
National Office
1700 North Moore Street, Suite 2000
Arlington, VA 22209
703.527.4126
http://www.youthventure.org

Youthwork Links and Ideas
Maine Youthwork
Barbara Kawliche
5 Ernest Street
Lewiston, ME 04240
email: comments@youthwork.com
http://www.youthwork.com
http://www.youthwork.com/maine

Visit http://www.youthleadership.com for updates to this list.

Youth Leadership Conferences/Programs

Adelante Mujer (Onward Woman) Latina Leadership Conference
Women at Work
50 N. Hill Avenue, Suite 300
Pasadena, CA 91106
626.796.6870 (x29 or x31)
email: adelantelatina@womenatwork1.org
http://www.adelantemujerlatina.org/

AmeriCorps*NCCC (National Civilian Community Corps)
1201 New York Avenue, NW
Washington, DC 20525
202.606.5000
http://www.americorps.org

Arizona Collegiate Leadership Conference
Center for Student Involvement & Leadership
University of Arizona
Tucson, AZ 85721-0017
520.626.1572
email: aclc@email.arizona.edu
http://www.union.arizona.edu/csil/aclc/

Asian Pacific Youth Leadership Project
P.O. Box 22423
Sacramento, CA 95822
916.497.0776
http://www.apylp.org

Black Issues Forum
Colorado State University
Office of Admissions
8020 Campus Delivery
Fort Collins, CO 80523-8020
970.491.6909
http://lib.colostate.edu/research/divandarea/bif/

Boys State
The American Legion (In Your Area)
http://www.legion.org/?section=prog_evt&subsection=evt_bs&content=evt_bs

Choose To Lead, Inc.
153 Frederick Street, Suite 119
Kitchener, Ontario
Canada N2H 2M2
email: info@choosetolead.com
http://www.choosetolead.com

City Year
285 Columbus Avenue
Boston, MA 02116
617.927.2500
http://www.cityyear.org

Colorado Leadership Conference
University of Colorado at Boulder
400 Norlin Library
Campus Box 363
Boulder, CO 80309
303.492.8342
email: Barbara.Volpe@colorado.edu
http://www.colorado.edu/academics/plc/CLC.html

Congressional Youth Leadership Council (CYLC)
Includes:
- National Young Leaders Conference
- Global Young Leaders Conference
- Junior National Young Leaders Conference
- National Young Leaders State Conference
- Presidential Youth Inaugural Conference
- Junior Presidential Youth Inaugural Conference
- Global Young Leader's Summit

1110 Vermont Avenue, NW, Suite 320
Washington, DC 20005
202.638.0008
email: cylc@cylc.org
http://www.cylc.org

The Duke of Edinburgh's Award
Young Canadians Challenge
Suite 450
207 Queen's Quay West
PO Box 124
Toronto, Ontario
M5J 1A7
416.203.0674
email: national@dukeofed.org
http://www.dukeofed.org

Girl Power
email: gpower@health.org
http://www.girlpower.gov/

G.U.T.S. "Guys & Gals Utilizing Their Strengths"
7816 Williams Moyers Avenue
Albuquerque, NM 87122
505.797.0961
email: questions@presentation-style.com
http://www.presentation-style.com/guts

Hugh O'Brian Youth Leadership
10880 Wilshire Boulevard
Suite 410
Los Angeles, CA 90024
310.474.4370 x 249
email: hoby@hoby.org
http://www.hoby.org

LeaderShape Institute
1802 Fox Drive, Suite D
Champaign, IL 61820
800.988.LEAD
217.351.6200
email: lead@leadershape.org
http://www.leadershape.org

Lideres - Youth Leadership Summit
National Council of La Raza
1111 19th Street NW, Suite 1000
Washington, DC 20036
800.311.NCLR
202.785.1670
email: leadership@nclr.org
http://www.nclr.org

National Association of the Deaf
Youth Leadership Camp
814 Thayer Avenue
Silver Spring, MD 20910
301.587.1788
301.587.1789 TTY
email: nadyouth@nad.org
email: YLCdirector@nad.org
http://www.nad.org/YLC/

National Association of Secondary School Principals (NASSP)
National Association of Student Councils (NASC)
LEAD conferences throughout academic year
1904 Association Drive
Reston, VA 20191-1537
703.860.0200
800.253.7746
email: dsa@principals.org
http://www.nasc.us/s_nasc/index.asp

National Resource Center for Youth Services
University of Oklahoma
202 W. 8th Street
Tulsa, OK 74119-1419
918.585.2986 x 230
email: sschelbar@ou.edu
http://www.nrcys.ou.edu

National Student Leadership Conference
Office of Admissions
111 West Jackson Boulevard, 7th Floor
Chicago, IL 60604
800.994.6752 (in continental US)
312.322.9999 (outside continental US)
email: info@NSLCleaders.org
http://www.nslcleaders.org
http://www.nslcinfo.org

National Teen Leadership Program (NTLP)
2443 Fair Oaks Blvd., #342
Sacramento CA 95825
800.550.1950
916.941.3886
email: info@teenleader.org
http://www.teenleader.org

National Youth Leadership Council (NYLC)
1910 W. County Road B
St. Paul, MN 55113
651.631.3672
email: nylcinfo@nylc.org
http://www.nylc.org

National Youth Leadership Forum
Includes:
- National Youth Leadership Forum on Defense, Intelligence and Diplomacy (202.777.4002)
- National Youth Leadership Forum on Law (202.777.4003)
- National Youth Leadership Forum on Medicine (202.628.6090)
- National Youth Leadership Forum on Technology (202.777.4100)
- National Youth Leadership Forum on Nursing (202.777.0581)

1110 Vermont Avenue, N.W., Suite 330
Washington, DC 20005
email: info@nylf.org
http://www.nylf.org

New Light Leadership Coalition, Inc.
P.O. Box 66305
Baltimore, MD 21239-6305
866.655.2462
email: info@nllc.org
http://www.nllc.org

Ohio Leadership Institute
5330 E. Main Street, Suite 207
Columbus, OH
888.878.LEAD
email: ohioleader@aol.com
http://www.OhioLeader.com

Outward Bound School
Various experiences
800.477.2627
http://www.outwardboundwilderness.org/

Path of Success, Inc.
Choate Rosemary Hall
333 Christian Street
Wallingford, CT 06492
877.898.7284
email: psa@pathofsuccess.org
http://www.pathofsuccess.org

PeaceJam
2427 West Argyle Place
Denver, CO 80211
303.455.2099
http://www.peacejam.org

Points of Light Youth Leadership Institute
Points of Light Foundation
1400 I ("Eye") Street, NW, Suite 800
Washington, DC 20005
202-729-8000
email: Info@PointsofLight.org
http://www.pyli.org/

Presidential Classroom
119 Oronoco Street
Alexandria, VA 22314-2015
800.441.6533
703.683.5400
email: PrezClass@aol.com
http://www.PresidentialClassroom.org

Prudential Spirit of Community/Youth Leadership Program
c/o NASSP
800.253.7746
http://www.prudential.org/community/spirit/

Public Leadership Education Network (PLEN)
Preparing Women to Lead (college/university-age programs)
1001 Connecticut Avenue NW, Suite 900
Washington, DC 20036
202.872.1585
email: plen@plen.org
http://www.plen.org

Tennessee Youth Leadership Forum for Students with Disabilities
Cordell Hull Building
425 5th Avenue North
Nashville, TN 37243
email: nsolomon@mail.state.tn.us
http://www.tennessee.gov/cdd/ylf.html

The High School Environmental Leadership Training Program
Sierra Student Coalition
Summer Program May Application Deadline
P.O. Box 2402 Conferences Late July/Early
Providence, RI 02906 August
404.861.6012 (Vermont & California Locations)
email: ssc-info@ssc.org
http://www.ssc.org/

The Leading Edge @ High Mountain Institute
PO Box 970
Leadville, CO 80461
ph: 719.486.8200
email: kbartlett@hminet.org
http://www.hminet.org/page.php?pname=edge

United States Senate Youth Program
Nelma Hundley
Senate Youth Program Coordinator
Colorado Department of Education
201 East Colfax Avenue
Denver, CO 80203-1799
303.866.6865
email: hundley_n@cde.state.co.us
http://www.cde.state.co.us/cdeawards/senateyouth.htm

Volunteer Toronto
416.961.6888
http://www.volunteertoronto.on.ca/yintro.asp

Women's Foundation of Colorado
1901 East Asbury Avenue
Denver, CO 80208
303.285.2960
http://www.wfco.org

Youth2Work
U.S. Department of Labor
Frances Perkins Building
200 Constitution Avenue, NW
Washington, DC 20210
866.487.2365
http://www.youth2work.gov/

Youth Leadership Camps Canada (YLCC)
Leadership Innovations Inc.
81 Ridout Street
London, Ontario, Canada N6C 1X8
519.438.4800
email: stusaunders@ylcc.com
http://www.ylcc.com

Youth Leadership Forum for Students with Disabilities
Office of Disability Employment Policy
1331 F Street, NW
Washington, DC 20004
Telephone: 202.693.7880
email: epstein-alicia@dol.gov
http://www.dol.gov/odep/programs/ylf.htm

Youth Leadership for Vital Communities Initiative
c/o Center for 4-H Youth Development
270 B McNamara Alumni Center
200 Oak Street SE
Minneapolis, MN 55455
612.624.7988
http://www.ylvc.org

Youth Leadership Institute
246 First Street, Suite 400
San Francisco, CA 94150
415.836.9160
email: info@yli.org
http://www.yli.org

Youth Leadership Initiative
University of Virginia Center for Politics
2400 Old Ivy Road
P.O. Box 400806
Charlottesville, VA 22904
866.514.8389
email: ylihelp@virginia.edu
http://www.youthleadership.net

Youth Service America
1101 15th Street, NW, Suite 200
Washington, DC 20005
202.296.2992
email: info@ysa.
http://www.ysa.org

Youth Venture
1700 N. Moore Street, Suite 2000
Arlington, VA 22209
703.527.4126
email: info@youthventure.org
http://www.youthventure.org

Visit http://www.youthleadership.com for updates to this list.

Professional Development Opportunities

America's Promise
909 N. Washington Street, Suite 400
Alexandria, VA 22314-1556
703.684.4500
http://www.americaspromise.org

Association for Experiential Education
2305 Canyon Blvd., Suite 100
Boulder, CO 80302-5651
303.440.8844
http://www.aee.org

Center for Creative Leadership
P.O. Box 26300
Greensboro, NC 27438-6300
336.545.2810
http://www.ccl.org

Center for Leadership Studies
Our Lady of the Lake University
411 S.W. 24th Street
San Antonio, TX 78207
210.434.6711
http://www.ollusa.edu/academic/secs/LeadershipStudies/

Community Partnerships with Youth, Inc.
550 E. Jefferson Street, Suite 306
Franklin, IN 46131
317.736.7947
http://www.cpyinc.org

Eureka! Performance Group
707.279.1676
email: info@eurekaperformance.com
http://www.eurekaperformance.com

Executive Edge, Inc.
46 Chagrin Plaza, #147
Chagrin Falls, OH 44022
800.632.3343
email: info@executiveedgeinc.com
http://www.executiveedgeinc.com

Fulbright Academic Exchange Program
(Graduate School Opportunities)
212.984.5330
http://www.iie.org/fulbright

Gardner Carney Leadership Institute
Fountain Valley School of Colorado
6155 Fountain Valley School Road
Colorado Springs, CO 80911
719.390.7035 x233
email: gcli@fvs.edu
http://www.fvs.edu/gcli/default.asp

International Leadership Association
Academy of Leadership
College Park, MD 20742-7715
301.405.5218
email: ila@academy.umd.edu
http://www.academy.umd.edu/ila

The James MacGregor Burns Academy of Leadership
University of Maryland
1107 Taliaferro Hall
College Park, MD 20742-7715
301.405.5751
http://www.academy.umd.edu

Jepson School of Leadership Studies
28 Westhampton Way
University of Richmond, VA 23173
804.287.6086
http://oncampus.richmond.edu/academics/leadership/academics/FAQ.html

National Association for Campus Activities (NACA)
13 Harbison Way
Columbia, SC 29212-3401
803.732.6222
http://www.naca.org

The Community Leadership Association
200 S. Meridian Street, Suite 250
Indianapolis, IN 46225
800.553.2337
http://www.communityleadership.org

National Association of Student Activity Advisors/National Association of Secondary School Principals (NASAA/NASSP)
1904 Association Drive
Reston, VA 20191
Student Council advisor resources and training
800.253.7746
http://www.nassp.org

National Clearinghouse for Leadership Programs (NCLP)
1135 Stamp Union
University of Maryland
College Park, MD 20742-7174
301.405.0799
http://www.nclp.umd.edu

National Community for Latino Leadership (NCLL)
4539 North 22nd Street, Suite 202
Phoenix, AZ 85016-4661
http://www.latinoleadership.org

National Center for NonProfit Boards National Leadership Forum (NCNB)
2000 L Street, NW Suite 510
Washington, DC 20036
800-883-6262
http://www.ncnb.org

National Council of La Raza
1111 19th Street NW, Suite 1000
Washington, DC 20036
800.311.NCLR
email: info@nclr.org
http://www.nclr.org

National Foundation for Teaching Entrepreneurship
NFTE-Greater Washington
733 15th Street NW, Suite 300
Washington, DC 20005
202.628.NFTE
http://www.nfte.com

National Hispana Leadership Institute
1901 North Moore Street, Suite 206
Arlington, VA 22209-1706
703.527.6007
http://www.nhli.org

National Youth at Risk Conference
Division of Continuing Education & Public Services
P.O. Box 8124
Georgia Southern University
Statesboro, GA 30460-8124
912.681.5555
http://ceps.georgiasouthern.edu/conted/nationalyouthatrisk.html

National Youth Leadership Council (NYLC)
1910 W. County Road B
St. Paul, MN 55113
651.631.3672
nylcinfo@nylc.org
912-681-5555
http://www.nylc.org

Points of Light Foundation
1400 Street, NW Suite 800
Washington, DC 20005
202-729-8000
http://www.pointsoflight.org
http://www.pyli.org/certified.html

Project Adventure (4 offices nationwide)
Experiential Education training/Ropes Course Certification
800.468.8898
email: info@pa.org
http://www.pa.org/

Public Allies
1015 18th Street NW, Suite 200
Washington, DC 20036
202.822.1180
http://www.publicallies.org

The Aspen Institute
1333 New Hampshire Avenue, NW
Suite 1070
Washington, DC 20036
202.736.5800
800.410.3463 (Events)
http://www.aspeninst.org

Think Like A Genius, LLC
4950 S. Yosemite Street,
Suite F2-325
Greenwood Village, CO 80111
303.649.9388
email: tsiler@thinklikeagenius.com
http://www.thinklikeagenius.com/highband/index.html

W.K. Kellogg Foundation
One Michigan Avenue East
Battle Creek, MI 49017-4058
616.968.1611
http://www.wkkf.org/default.aspx

The Woodrow Wilson School of Public & International Affairs
Princeton University, Robertson Hall
Princeton, NJ 08544
609.258.4836
email: WWSAdmit@princeton.edu
http://www.wws.princeton.edu

Youth Leadership (Youth Ministry Education/Training Program)
122 W. Franklin Avenue
Suite 510
Minneapolis, MN 55404
612.870.3632
email: info@youthleadership.org
http://www.youthleadership.org

Youth Leadership Initiative
University of Virginia Center for Politics
2400 Old Ivy Road, P.O. Box 400806
Charlottesville, VA 22904
866.514.8389
email: ylihelp@virginia.edu
http://www.youthleadership.net

Movies to Watch/Use for Leadership Discussions*

(In Alphabetical Order)

A Bug's Life
A League of Their Own
All The President's Men
Apollo 13
A River Runs Through It
Boys in the Hood
Bring It On
Charlotte's Web
Circle of Friends
Dances With Wolves
Dead Poets Society
Driving Miss Daisy
Dune
Erin Brockovich
Firehouse Dog
Gandhi
G.I. Jane
Good Will Hunting
Higher Learning
Independence Day
JFK
Last of the Mohicans
Malcolm X
Norma Rae
Remains of the Day
Romy & Michelle's High School Reunion
Schindler's List
Shawshank Redemption
Sling Blade
Sneakers
Stand and Deliver
Steal Big Steal Little
The Breakfast Club
The Candidate
The Cider House Rules
The Godfather
The Joy Luck Club
The Mighty Ducks
The Outsiders
The Red Sneakers
The Spitfire Grill
Toy Story
Twelve Angry Men
Wall Street
What's Eating Gilbert Grape
Willy Wonka and the Chocolate Factory

A Few Good Men
All the King's Men
Amistad
Arthur and the Invisibles
Bill and Ted's Excellent Adventure
Braveheart
Chariots of Fire
Chicken Run
Cry Freedom
Dave
Dinosaur
Drumline
Empire Records
Evita
Fried Green Tomatoes
Gettysburg
Glory
Grease
Hudsucker Proxy
Jakob the Liar
King of the Hill
Lord of the Flies
Mr. Holland's Opus
October Sky
Rescue Heroes: The Movie
Rudy
Selena
Simon Birch
Smoke Signals
Snow Dogs
Stand By Me
The American President
The Browning Version
The Chocolate War
The Color Purple
The Hobbit
The Lion King
The Milagro Beanfield War
The Princess Bride
The Rookie
The Stone of Cold Fire
Top Gun
Vision Quest
Watership Down
With Honors
Wizard of Oz

*(G/PG/PG-13/R)

Leadership Action Plan

My leadership goal is:

_____
_____
_____

The first action I will take to achieve this goal is:

_____
_____
_____

The people who will help or support me are:

_____ _____ _____

The things or people which (who) may get in my way are:

_____ _____ _____

I will be ready to deal with these things by:

_____
_____
_____

I will know I have achieved my goal when:

_____
_____
_____

I will check my progress on the following dates:

_____ _____ _____

This goal will be accomplished by the following date: _____

Designing Student Leadership Programs
Copyright © 2000 Mariam MacGregor
3rd Edition, 2005

Leadership Project Evaluation

Group & Self Evaluation

(Each member of the group should fill out evaluations
for the other members as individuals, and for yourself).

Please Rate each of your group members, including yourself on the following areas:

1 = Poor, Really did not contribute
2 = Okay, Had good days and bad, depending on the responsibilities
3 = Good, For the most part, followed through and helped the group
4 = Fabulous, Always did this!

Name of Person you Are Rating: _____

Your Name: _____

1. Contributed to group ideas _____

2. Showed Initiative when asked to do something _____

3. Communicated well and kept others informed _____

4. Delegated Responsibility _____

5. Able to take on multiple tasks and balance priorities _____

6. Respected differences of opinion and helped the group work through difficulties _____

7. Consistently worked toward our mutual goal _____

8. Challenged me to do my best as a group member _____

9. Had an accurate perception of his/her own strengths/weaknesses _____

10. Positively represented characteristics of a good leader _____

Add All for Total: _____

About The Author

Mariam is a former school counselor and founded and runs Youthleadership.com, a website resource center for individuals working with youth leaders. The website connects thousands around the world with information and links that can assist in creating meaningful leadership opportunities for teens and young adults.

After working with college student leaders at Syracuse University, Santa Clara University and Metropolitan State College of Denver, Mariam chose secondary education to integrate "best-learned practices" and innovative approaches from higher education to leadership development with adolescents. Mariam served as school counselor/coordinator of leadership programs at Vantage Point Campus Alternative High School. While there, she received Honorable Mention as "Counselor of the Year" for the State of Colorado.

Her curriculum, *Building Everyday Leadership in All Teens* and accompanying teen guidebook, *Everyday Leadership: Attitudes and Actions for Respect and Success* (Free Spirit Publishing, 2007) is widely used in school and community settings. Her newest book, *Teambuilding with Teens: Activities for Leadership, Decision Making and Group Success* (Free Spirit Publishing, 2008) presents 36 interactive, hands-on activities for use with all teens. Mariam is a contributing curriculum developer for the Girl Scouts USA National Leadership Launch journeys (2008).

Over the years, Mariam has consulted with organizations and presented workshops to diverse audiences, emphasizing ways to design meaningful and sustainable youth leadership experiences, regardless of setting. She has written articles on youth leadership for various publications and is available for trainings. Mariam writes from the foothills outside Denver, Colorado, where she lives with her husband and kids.